THE END OF THE WORLD

Shaykh Muhammad Mitwalli Al-Sha'rawi

DAR AL TAQWA LTD.

© Dar Al Taqwa Ltd. 2001

ISBN 1 870582 46 2

Translation: Aisha Bewley

Editors: Abdalhaqq Bewley, Muhammad Isa Waley

Production: Bookwork, Norwich

Published by:
Dar Al Taqwa Ltd.
7A Melcombe Street
Baker Street
London NW1 6AE

Printed and bound by :
Deluxe Printers
245a, Acton Lane,London NW10 NR
Tel. : 020 8965 1771
email : de-luxe@talk21.com

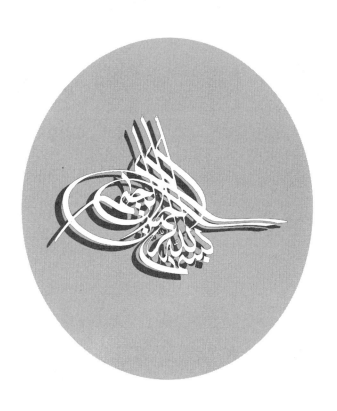

Table of Contents

Chapter One
The Changing and the Immutable

The question of the end of the world has captured the interest of scientists, false prophets, charlatans and others, each of whom attempts to make predictions about the day or time when the world we live in will end. All the scientific theories which have been or will be articulated are based on guesswork and supposition, not actual knowledge. That is because human knowledge, owing to its limited capacity, will never be able to arrive at any certainty on this subject. Man's knowledge of space is still in its infancy. The latest discoveries of mankind indicate that there are stars and suns millions of light years from earth, or further still. What we know is only very minimal compared to what we do not know about this vast universe.

Allah Almighty informs us in the Noble Qur'an that "heaven" refers to all that is above us:

"As for heaven – We built it with great power and gave it its vast expanse." (51:47)

The vastness here refers to Allah's power, not the power of mankind. That is why, whenever scientists believe that they have plumbed the depths of the universe, some new discovery contradicts what they have previously proclaimed and opens up new horizons for them. Theories change every few months, proving to those scientists that they had only imagined that they had arrived at the truth. The truth is that they have not arrived at anything.

When we observe fortune-tellers and charlatans, we find that every year or every few years they prophesy that the end of the world will occur on a certain day. Astonishingly, a large number of people continue to believe them even though their predictions are not based on any actual knowledge or science. In America one false prophet recently predicted that the world would come to an end on a certain day, and some people believed him. They left their homes and climbed the highest mountain thinking that they would be saved. Naturally, the day passed and nothing happened and so people knew that they had been duped. Others, as we know, kill themselves whilst under a similar delusion.

There are dozens of fortune-tellers who make strange prophecies about the end of the world, all of which are false, not being based on any knowledge or understanding. They are simply a swindle with the aim of making money from those duped by false claims. The appointed time for the end of the world is known only to Allah Almighty. It has a time which the Almighty has stipulated but He has not informed anyone about it, even the angels.

Before continuing, we must mention here the changing and the immutable. The immutable is the universe which Allah Almighty created for the sake of man. Allah made this vast universe of heaven and earth and what is between them subservient to man. It performs the task which has Allah has willed for it in a stable, unchanging way. But human beings, for whose sake the universe was created, are in constant fluctuation. The human being changes from strength to weakness, from health to illness, from capacity to incapacity, from life to death, from sanity to insanity. There are many variables in the lives of people as they move from one state to another, but this is not the case with the universe, whose nature is unchanging and immutable.

When we look at the changes to which mankind is subject, we find that the laws which govern them are laws which we do not understand. A human being moves from health to illness, from strength to incapacity, from life to death. These are changes whose occurrence follows no law of which we are aware. We cannot be certain as to when a human being will move from health to illness. If we knew how to determine the laws governing these things, perhaps we should be able to prevent or control them; but the laws are hidden from us despite all that scientists say. When, for instance, someone is afflicted by a blood clot in the brain, angina pectoris, or any other such disorder, science can do no more to predict it than apply the law of probability based on statistical analysis. But this provides nothing more than a speculative guess which is not founded on scientific fact.

In the same way, for instance, a human being may pass from wealth to poverty, or from poverty to wealth. There is no known law governing this phenomenon. It is the same with the all the changes which occur in our lives. Nor does a human being know when he will leave this world. He may be in the best of health and fall down dead in an instant, or he may be chronically ill and yet live for many years. The question arises why man is subject to such unpredictable changes when all that was created for him has immutable laws which do not change. The answer is that this universe was created to provide mankind with the components necessary for life. It was not created for one single generation so as to end when that generation ended: it was created for all the generations of mankind until the Day of Rising. That is why generation after generation receives the same gifts subject to the same universal laws.

From the time of Adam until now, when a seed is placed in the earth, watered and cared for and free of any diseases which may affect it, it produces its fruits. Since the time of Adam until now, the earth has never refused to give its fruits to a single generation. It does not say, "I will give fruit to this generation and deny it to the generation after it." From the time of Adam until now, the sun rises according to a fixed pattern and sets according to a fixed pattern. We do not know of it giving its rays to one generation and denying them to another. It is the same with rain, wind and other elements of life: they are given to every generation and do not fail to fulfil their function at any time. That is indicated by the words of the Allah Almighty:

3

"The sun and the moon both run with precision." (55:5)

This means that they follow a precise pattern which never varies.

So creation contains both what has been created and something for which those things have been created. That something for which all other things have been created is the human being, and we see the human being changes and moves from one state to another. This is an actual fact which we witness daily. So, within the framework of his life, a human being passes through many states and situations and then there is another great change when he is annihilated through death. These changes have no defined limits or times. They are subject to laws which are hidden from us.

Man and the Laws of Change

Throughout his lifetime a human being changes every day. He is subject to laws about which we know nothing. He is subject to one law while he is awake and another law, about which we know almost nothing, while asleep. When someone sleeps he sees things which are not amenable to any logic. He sees himself speaking to people who have died long ago, or falls from the top of a mountain with no adverse consequences, or travels to the ends of the earth and back again in a few minutes. He sees, although his eyes are closed. He walks, although his feet remain on his bed. He speaks, yet his tongue is still and unmoving. All of this happens in a single instant. A human being moves from the laws governing wakefulness to the laws governing sleep in a moment. This shows us that relocating a human being from one set of laws to another which is completely different is a simple operation for Allah Almighty. When we read the Noble Qur'an we find that Allah Almighty says:

"Allah takes back people's souls when their death arrives, and those who have not yet died while they are asleep. He keeps hold of those whose death has been decreed and sends the others back for a specified term. There are certainly signs in that for people who reflect." (39:42)

So man's movement from wakefulness to sleep is comparable to his movement from life to death. Despite the similarities, the laws governing each state are different. The soul of the sleeper returns to his body when he wakes up but when the soul is taken in death, will only be returned to its body on the Day of Resurrection. The Messenger of Allah, may Allah bless him and grant him peace, said:

"By the One who has my soul in His hand, you will die as you sleep and you will be resurrected as you wake up. You will be called to Reckoning for what you used to do and you will be repaid with good for good and evil for evil. That means a Garden forever or a Fire forever."

When someone dies, he sees, at the moment of his death, what a sleeping person does not see. He sees the angels and he sees what was previously hidden from him and knows whether he is going to the Garden or the Fire. This movement from one set of laws to another takes place without any human being knowing how it is reached. This change, from one state to another and then the return to the first state, are all laws which we do not understand, even though they happen to us and affect every one of us.

When we look at all existence, we find that the universe operates in a manner which is beneficial to us but we do not know how it operates. The rain, for instance, is a provision for all of those on the earth, they drink from the water it brings, and it is the basis of all life, as Allah Almighty tells us:

"And We made from water every living thing." (21:30)

Yet a person can live without ever knowing how rain is formed. He does not need to know how vapour is sucked up from the oceans and then becomes clouds in the upper atmosphere and then falls as rain. But does the fact that a person does not know how the rain comes prevent him from having it to drink and water his crops and flocks and other things? No, it does not. Even today there is no difference between those who know how rain falls and those who do not, in respect of their use of the water it brings. There are those who know and those who do not know, but they all use the rain water. It is the same with the sun, air and earth: whether their secrets and laws are known or not, they are still made use of.

Scientists have gone to great lengths to delve into the secrets of the universe. Allah Almighty wished to disclose to them some of the secrets of existence, which has increased their knowledge of the laws that Allah has set in place in the universe which He created. These laws make life much easier for man and reduce the amount of effort he must expend to survive. In the past, a man went to a well to get water; now he has water in his house and only needs to turn on a tap to get it. This is progress in the utilisation of resources but man did not bring about the existence of the resources he uses.

The intellect and scientific discoveries

Gravity, for instance, has fulfilled its role from the day Allah Almighty created the universe; but man only learned of it comparatively recently. Man's ignorance of gravity did not prevent it fulfilling its role. Airwaves transmit sounds and other things. All such things serve man without him necessarily knowing about them or their laws. To give you a clearer idea of this, imagine that you go to an illiterate man and tell him, "If you want elec-

6

tric light to illuminate this place, then press this switch. If you want to watch television programmes, turn this knob." Does the ignorance of this illiterate man prevent him from using the electric light or watching television? It does not. Whenever he wants light, he presses the light switch and whenever he wants to watch television, he turns the knob. His lack of understanding of the secrets and laws of electricity or the secrets of television broadcasting and the manner of its transmission does not prevent him from utilising such devices.

The same applies to existence as a whole – and will continue to do so. When the human intellect investigates and Allah discloses to it some of His phenomena in existence, man progresses by desiring benefit from his discoveries and turning them to his own use. Things which used to require great effort and take a long time are now achieved with a minimum of effort and in a short time. A person once had to carry a bushel of grain on his back and endure much toil to transport things from one place to another, but this toil all but disappeared thanks to the discovery of the wheel. Transport then developed rapidly, and then science progressed to where we are now, with modern devices which require little time and effort, and man is spared a great deal of toil.

But do these inventions and this scientific progress bring into existence anything which did not already exist in the earth? Certainly not. Allah Almighty is the One who has brought everything in the universe into existence from the beginning of creation until the Day of Rising. However far human beings progress in their cultures, all they are doing is becoming acquainted with some of the Signs of Allah in existence which enable them to have a more comfortable life. Allah Almighty says:

> *"It is He who created everything on the earth for you."*
> (2:29)

7

Every day we see the power of the Creator to render His creatures powerless. However much man progresses in science and his intelligence develops, and however many secrets Allah discloses to him which were previously hidden, man cannot create anything new. He can only produce something from another thing which already exists. In spite of that, there are matters which some people think that man has a share in, such as agriculture and the improvement of plant and animal species, and other new discoveries which are put to the service of man, like his ability to fly, put artificial satellites into orbit, or land on the moon. These advances did not come out of nothing. They were accomplished through something which already existed but was hidden, from man, until the moment of its discovery.

In order to discover rocket propulsion, man studied the laws of the atmosphere and the laws of energy which the rocket requires. But did these laws not exist in the universe when Allah created it? Of course they existed, and they were part of Allah's creation from the first moment that Allah Almighty said to existence, "Be!". No one can claim, however much he knows, that he has produced a new atmospheric covering for the earth, or that he has altered or changed the composition of the atmosphere in order to be able to send a rocket into space, or that he has opened a door in the atmosphere around the earth in order to enable man to leave it and reach the moon. No one can claim that he has done any of those things. Allah Almighty is the One who created them all and brought them into existence in those forms and then He revealed them to man and taught him how to use them.

When human beings progress in their lives, their knowledge of the Signs of Allah in the existence He created is increased. That is why Allah Almighty says:

> "Only those of His slaves with knowledge have fear of Allah." (35:28)

Those with knowledge should have more fear of Allah because it is they who have recognised some of the Signs of Allah in His creation, Signs which attest to the immensity of the Creator and the exactitude of His fashioning. Yet instead of prostrating out of humility to the Immensity of Allah, scientists frequently talk about how they have discovered some of the secrets of existence as if they were the ones who brought them into existence! Allah Almighty says in His precise *ayat*:

> "*We will show them Our Signs on the horizon and within themselves until it is clear to them that it is the truth. Is it not enough for your Lord that He is a witness of everything?*"(41:53)

However much time passes, when we read the noble *ayat, "We will show them…"* it seems to refer to the Signs of Allah in existence and in His creation until the end of the world.

We should pause here for a moment to consider how the Path of Allah is put in place with astonishing precision to lead the human being to belief. Everything in this existence is set out with wisdom for the purpose of leading to faith and in the service of the Path of Allah. Allah Almighty chose the path of life for His creatures as well as providing them with evidence for belief in Him. Allah Almighty is invisible to us and we do not see Him, so a person might come and say, "I will not believe unless I see Him!" We tell him, "Do not be hasty. Existence is one thing, whereas perception of existence is something completely different."

Take, for example, the germs which kill people and bring about diseases. Have these germs not existed from the beginning of creation? Indeed, they existed, but we could not see them because of their very minute size. Yet they were always fulfilling their role in existence. They had many tasks even if we knew nothing about them. Then science progressed: large microscopes were invented which magnified things hundreds or thousands of times, and we discovered these germs. They are very minute

9

creatures which have their own special laws and life cycles, by which they reproduce and multiply. They can penetrate our skins without our feeling them and they can enter the blood vessels and pass through an incubation period in the blood stream. They multiply and there are battles between them and our white blood cells. These are things which we now know since we discovered them and learned about them.

Were these germs created at the moment when we observed them? Of course not. They have existed since the beginning of creation but we did not know or perceive their existence until recently. The same applies to everything in existence, for example, the airwaves which carry sounds and pictures to all corners of the earth in seconds, so that you can sit at home and watch a man land on the moon at the very moment he does it, or watch an important event while it is actually taking place and yet, sitting in your room and the event is happening thousands of miles away.

Does man add a special quality to the air which enables it to convey sound and pictures around the world in seconds? The answer is, of course, no. The air has always existed as Allah Almighty created it, with all its properties but we did not discover this particular property until very recently, just as we discovered that it can support aeroplanes regardless of their size and the weight they carry. All these special qualities have existed in the universe since Allah created it, but we did not discover them until Allah gave us permission to do so. Then they became evident to us and we recognised them and made use of them. This has happened because everything in existence has been put at the service of man.

If anyone should come and say, "We cannot see God, so how can we believe in Him?" we would tell him that Allah Almighty has provided us with evidence in existence which allows us to know with certainty that many things exist which we cannot see, even if we do not know directly of their existence. The point of this is that science should serve faith and make it easier for us to believe in Allah. Whenever Allah discloses something to us, we should say, "Glory be to Allah who created, originated and fashioned!". But instead of using science to strengthen our faith we tend to believe that we have reached these things by ourselves, that we are the ones who brought them into existence, that they are the results of our own efforts. We attribute them to mankind rather than ascribing them to their Almighty Creator. People have begun to use science to fight faith while in reality science only affirms the existence of Allah.

Divine Power versus human power

This is one of the great tragedies of the world in which we live. We see all those unchanging phenomena in existence which have served man generation after generation without any effort on the part of humanity and without us knowing anything about their laws. But now reality has been turned on its head and we have begun to claim that we are in control of the universe. We claim that we ourselves have subdued the earth by our own efforts and we make it produce crops for us by our own efforts. Indeed, we go even further and discredit the five hidden things mentioned in the Qur'an as known only to Allah, claiming instead that they have been disclosed to man. Allah says:

> "Truly Allah has knowledge of the Hour and sends down abundant rain and knows what is in the wombs. And no soul knows what it will earn tomorrow and no soul knows in what land it will die. Allah is All-Knowing, All-Aware." (31:34)

Yet you find people standing in front of television cameras insinuating that it is man who makes the rain fall, even though rain falls without any action on our part. No one can claim that he is the one who makes the rays of sunlight fall on the oceans so that water vapour rises to the upper layers of the atmosphere, nor can anyone say that he is the one who makes this water condense into clouds. No one can claim that he issues commands to the wind to move these clouds to the place where Allah has decreed that the rain will fall, nor can anyone say that he makes clouds strike cold mountain peaks and snow. All of this process is accomplished without us having any part in it. Read the words of Allah Almighty:

"It is He who sends out the winds, bringing advance news of His mercy, so that when they have lifted up the heavy clouds, We dispatch them to a dead land and send down water to it, by means of which We bring forth all kinds of fruit. In the same way We will bring forth the dead, so that hopefully you will pay heed." (7:57)

By His power, Allah Almighty produces the clouds and He is the One who drives them wherever He wishes. He says:

"Do you not see that Allah propels the clouds, then makes them coalesce, then heaps them up, and then you see the rain come pouring from the middle of them? And He sends down mountains from the sky with hail inside them, striking with it anyone He wills and averting it from anyone He wills. The brightness of His lightning almost blinds the sight. Allah revolves the night and day. There is surely a lesson in that for people with eyes." (24:43)

Invisible things and human changeability

Allah Almighty tells us in the Noble Qur'an of the unchanging realities of the rain cycle. Because science has discovered that rain can be produced by seeding clouds with a chemical substance, some people have deluded themselves into claiming that they can make it rain and that one of the five invisible matters which Allah alone knows has therefore been revealed.

But what part do we play in rainfall? It is an awesome and immense process, from its beginning when the vapour rises from the oceans to the point when the rain falls. Even if everyone in the entire world were to help one another, they would still not be able to make a single drop of rain fall. If man were really able to make the rain fall, he would have watered the deserts so that they could produce crops. If it were possible to move the clouds to another place, people living in places which suffer from floods would be spared and arid areas would be green.

Allah Almighty sends down rain from heaven, from which all people, their flocks and herds and other living things drink. Allah created rivers which extend for thousands of kilometres. Can science produce for us one small canal full of water in the middle of the desert? It is sad that instead of using science in a sound manner in the service of faith people put it to the service of disbelief and atheism, and instead of ascribing what is in existence to the power of Allah Almighty people ascribe it to themselves and their own powers.

To summarise, Allah created all phenomenal existence to serve mankind and it is firm and unchanging in its patterns. Man changes from one state to another by laws which are hidden from us and unknown to us. Allah Almighty created all the phenomena in the universe to serve the cause of faith, but man has made them serve disbelief and atheism.

Chapter Two
The Beginning and the End

The existence of Allah Almighty alone is without beginning or end. Every creature that He created necessarily has a beginning and an end. All existence and whatever and whoever is in it, has a beginning and an end. When the Last Day comes then everything in this universe will be annihilated – sun, moon, stars, earth, mountains and seas. On this subject, Allah Almighty says in the Noble Qur'an:

> *"On the Day the earth is changed to other than the earth, and the heavens likewise, and they parade before Allah, the One, the Conquering."* (14:48)

That is how Allah Almighty informs us in the Noble Qur'an that when the Day of Resurrection and Final Gathering comes, the earth on which we live will be destroyed and a new earth will appear – the earth of the appointed Gathering on which all mankind will be brought together and summoned to the Reckoning. We will emerge from our graves on this new earth and we will be driven to the appointed Gathering.

We, as believers, know for certain that there will be an end to the life of this world, followed by a new beginning. However, there are those who try to create doubts about this and claim that there is nothing after death. None of those who presently embrace that notion, such as existentialists, Communists and other atheists of all varieties, have done anything but repeat the ideas of the unbelievers of every previous age. Atheistic thought repeats itself and never progresses because it is founded on falsehood which re-iterates its claims in various forms but with nothing new in content. Read what Allah Almighty says:

> *"They say, 'There is nothing but our existence in this world. We die and we live and nothing destroys us but time.' They have no knowledge of that. They are only conjecturing."* (45:24)

If you examine every claim about this existence made by unbelievers in all their various theories and philosophies and so forth, you will find that they deny the Resurrection and reject the existence of Allah who created them, will make them die, and then will bring them back to life. The unbelievers have a vested interest in there being no Day of Reckoning because it is in their nature to give free rein to their lower impulses and appetites and do whatever they want. They hope that they will be able to steal, murder, lie, violate the honour of other people and commit perjury, and not suffer any adverse consequences! This is the greatest hope of every unbeliever. But it is a vain, false hope because on the Day of Rising Allah Almighty will call them to account for all the sins which they committed and the falsehoods which they embraced. Read the words of the Almighty:

> *"But the actions of those who reject are like a mirage in the desert. A thirsty man thinks it water, but when he reaches it he finds it nothing at all. But he finds Allah there and He will pay him his account in full. Allah is Swift at Reckoning."* (24:39)

This is the reality which every unbeliever denies but which will overtake him all of a sudden – and then all the riches of the world will not help him.

The human being and the elements of the earth

Before we speak about the end we should deal with the beginning in a general way, to see how Allah Almighty has provided the human being with evidence to make faith easy for him. The Almighty has given mankind a level playing field so that every human being has an equal opportunity to understand this evidence. The ability to understand it is not confined to those who have been given particular knowledge.

Allah Almighty created Adam from the elements of the earth. Scientific analysis has recently been carried out which proves that the body of the human being contains sixteen elements which are the same elements as those which exist in the earth. Thus we see that science has finally arrived at something that the Noble Qur'an disclosed fourteen centuries ago!

After Allah Almighty fashioned Adam with His hands, He breathed into him from His spirit and life flowed into his body. Then He created Eve from Adam's rib. Thus man is composed of both body and spirit. Allah left man to discover for himself the laws of the physical body over the passage of time, according to the knowledge he has acquired; but He made the Spirit a closed secret that man cannot uncover. All the research carried out to study the Spirit is useless because the Spirit is a mystery which can never be found out. The Spirit is not within the scope of scientific research: you cannot take it to a laboratory and carry out experiments on it in order to discover its laws.

Man has tried and will continue to try to discover something about it. A Swiss scientist performed an experiment in which he took a man who was on the point of death and placed him on a bed connected to a very precise scale. He found that at the moment of death when life left the body, the human being's weight decreased by a very small amount. After these experiments this scientist stated that the soul has a very small weight, not more than one hundredth of a gram. Many scientists deny that the soul exists at all and say that there is only time or nature.

Some of them resort to other philosophies and say that it is merely the life-force of the body. Allah Almighty says about this in His perfect Book:

"They will ask you about the Spirit. Say: 'The Spirit is my Lord's concern. You have only been given a little knowledge.'"
(17:85)

We should understand that there is the Spirit (*ruh*) and there is the body (*jasad*) and there is the experiencing self (*nafs*). The experiencing self is the meeting of the Spirit with matter, or the commingling of the Spirit and body. Responsibility imposed by Allah Almighty is not directed to the Spirit alone or to the body once the Spirit has left it. It applies when Spirit and body are associated together. That is in accordance with the words of the Almighty:

"By the self and what proportioned it and inspired it with depravity or godliness. He who purifies it has succeeded. He who buries it has failed." (91:8-10)

So we see that it is the experiencing self, which has existence during the time that the Spirit is mixed with matter, which is accountable for its actions. Punishment and bliss in the Hereafter will therefore be inflicted on the experiencing self. That is why Allah Almighty will reconstitute creation and will restore the bodies into which the souls will enter so that they are ready for the Reckoning. That is why we find that the *ayats* of the Noble Qur'an which speak about the Next World do not mention the Spirit alone or the body alone. They mention the experiencing self. Allah Almighty says:

*"Then every **self** will be paid in full for what it earned. They will not be wronged."* (2:161)

And He says:

17

*"Every **self** will come together with a driver and a witness."*
(50:21)

And He says:

*"Show fear of a Day when no **self** will be able to compensate for another in any way."* (2:48)

Thus we see that responsibility is directed to the self and punishment and bliss are dealt out to the self inasmuch as it is a mixture of Spirit and body or the commingling of matter and Spirit.

The nature of the Spirit

If asked to define the Spirit, we would say that it is a Divine secret which gives life to matter, or the will of Allah Almighty that we live. When Allah removes this will, life in its worldly form comes to an end. Death is not the end of the journey of life, it is the end of one stage during the journey and the beginning of a new one which has its own laws and life-form which Allah knows.

We have already seen, in the example of sleep, how man can move from one dimension to another in a single instant. When one lies on his bed and puts his head on his pillow, the instant he falls asleep he moves from a dimension where one set of laws apply to another dimension with different laws. When he wakes up again, he moves in that instant back from the law of sleep to the law of wakefulness, each completely different from the other.

The Messenger of Allah, may Allah bless him and grant him peace, explained to us that the life of this world is only a short period within the greater journey of life as a whole. In order to give us a precise picture of how short the time of our life in this world is in relation to the greater journey of life, he likened it to a traveller spending some time in the shade of a tree and then travelling on. The Prophet, may Allah bless him and grant him peace, said:

> "What have I to do with this world? There is no comparison between me and this world, except to a rider who stops for shade under a tree and then goes on leaving it behind."

Man knows nothing about the Spirit. The Jews asked the Messenger of Allah, may Allah bless him and grant him peace, about the Spirit and how it gives life to the body. They believed that the Messenger, peace and blessings be upon him, would tell them things from himself which they could use to attack the veracity of his Message, may Allah bless him and grant him peace. So Allah Almighty revealed:

> "They will ask you about the Spirit. Say: 'The Spirit is my Lord's concern. You have only been given a little knowledge.'"
> (17:85)

This means that the Spirit is one of the secrets of Allah Almighty which will remain hidden from us until the Day of Rising. But Allah made the Spirit, which is invisible to us, a guide to faith and a force which directs us to the power of Allah Almighty. It teaches us how to proceed on the Path of Faith while having complete certainty of the existence of Allah, Who caused existence to exist and created the universe and human life. Even though the Spirit is in the body of man, the person whose body it is in does not know anything about it and does not know how it came into his body or how it will leave. Nor does he know where in his body it is located.

Is it consciousness, which sends signals to the entire body so that life penetrates every part? Is it located in the heart, which beats when a human being is still a foetus in his mother's womb and continues to beat without any volition on our part until life comes to an end? Is it in the hand which strikes? Or in the foot which walks? Or in the eye which sees? Or in the ear which hears? Or the tongue which speaks? Where is the Spirit located?

"The Spirit is my Lord's concern"

The scientists who argue about Allah without having any real knowledge are incapable of perceiving the Spirit and its essence. They take empirical experience to be the boundary of all certain and actual knowledge. Such people try to cover up Allah's existence and profess disbelief and atheism; but that does not prevent the Spirit being in their bodies and with them during their sojourn in this world. If you were to ask them whether the Spirit exists or not they would reply categorically that it does, for the self-evident reason that the body is alive and not dead.

We say to them, "So the Spirit, which was created by Allah Almighty, certainly exists in your bodies and none of you can deny that. It definitely exists in every living thing. And yet in spite of that, you cannot see it or know what its composition is even though you observe its effects in your bodies. If you are incapable of perceiving the Spirit, how can you expect to see Allah Almighty? Why do you declare that the fact that you cannot see Allah Almighty is evidence that He does not exist? Have you not enough evidence from the experience of your own bodies which live with you through your life-journey to prove to you that you invent lies against Allah when you make those claims? If you truly understood, you would prostrate before the power of Allah Almighty, who has placed this incapacity in you in order to turn you towards the power of Allah and His immense knowledge."

But why has Allah Almighty concealed knowledge of the Spirit from mankind and not given mankind even a little understanding of it? There are a number of possible answers to this question: one, for instance, is so that we might perceive the immensity of the power of Allah and know for certain that it is this power, which is placed in the human body, which gives it life, even though no one is able to know anything specific about what imparts life to the body. When we observe that power, we are aware of the immensity of our Almighty and Magnificent Creator who placed this secret within us which we are unable to discover.

A second answer is that it provides us with proof of the fact that something can exist without there being any possibility of seeing it. That is evidence for the existence of things which we cannot see. We know with certainty that the Spirit is in our bodies by the very fact that we are alive. When the Spirit leaves, life stops. This enables us to be certain that the Unseen exists and of knowing that the fact that we cannot perceive it does not constitute evidence that it does not exist. With the case of the Spirit it is simply veiled from us so that we cannot see it but we can deduce its existence from its effects. The best testimony to the Unseen is the Spirit which inhabits our bodies. Allah Almighty says concerning this:

"... and in yourselves as well. Do you not then see?"

(51:21)

So man's perception of his own self provides him with evidence for belief in the existence of what is invisible to us and deduction of its existence through its effects. Is not this universe with all the forces it contains, which are greater than the powers of all mankind together, a decisive proof evidence for us of the existence of Allah Almighty?

Allah Almighty treats all His slaves equally. The existence of the Spirit in the body is something which does not require special knowledge. Everyone knows it because it lives with him and he lives with it. When doubt creeps into any human soul, it is enough for us to present the example of the Spirit to facilitate understanding in both the ignorant and the learned, those who read and write and those who have never read a single letter in their entire lives. Whether or not we know the reality of what this Life-force is, that does not increase or decrease the benefit derived from it. The benefit of the Spirit does not require knowledge: it gives life and power even if you know nothing about it.

Let us look further at the words of Allah Almighty:

"Say: 'The Spirit is my Lord's concern." (17:85)

What is the meaning of the words, *"my Lord's concern"*? How is this Spirit conveyed? Allah tells us in His words:

"His command when He desires a thing is just to say to it, 'Be' and it is." (36:82)

Hence the command of Allah – Glory be to Him and Exalted is He! – is His will in transferring the Spirit from His immediate presence to the life of the human being by the word "Be!" Therefore we must look at the words of the Almighty, *"He just says to it…".* The fact that Allah speaks to it shows that it must pre-exist in His knowledge which encompasses everything. So all the events in existence, from the beginning of creation and before creation – until the Day of Rising and after the Day of Rising – already exist.

There is a birth for everything in the knowledge of Allah Almighty. That is why when one of the gnostics was asked about the events which occur in people's lives, he said: "They are things which He makes manifest, not things which He originates from nothing." For all events in the life of this world pre-exist in Allah's knowledge: the Resurrection, the Reckoning, the Garden and the Fire. If Allah Almighty wished to disclose them to whomever He wished of His creation, He could do so. Read the words of the Almighty:

"Nothing occurs, either in the earth or in yourselves, without

its being in a Book before We make it happen. That is an easy matter for Allah." (57:22)

The events of this world and whatever events occur in the Next World are all in the knowledge of Allah Almighty, and issue forth from His knowledge to the knowledge of man by the word "Be!"; but man, as Allah describes him, *"is wrongdoing and ignorant"* (33:72). He is a wrongdoer because he is deluded and believes that the civilisations in which he lives were achieved by himself and on his own. In reality, he has not achieved anything except by using the intellect, power and substance which Allah created for him. Thereby Allah can disclose to man whichever of the laws of the universe He wishes which man then uses to raise his standard of living. Raising the standard of living only means that such a thing can be achieved in less time and with less effort.

In the past people used to climb stairs to reach upper floors and this was an arduous process in high buildings. Nowadays a lift takes us to the top floor in far less time and with far less effort. In the past when we wanted to go to a place, we had to walk or ride to it. Now we go by car, plane and other means of modern transport with less effort and in less time. The problem is that when man sees this scientific progress he tends to worship this world. This means that he is ignorant – very ignorant indeed. He forgets that Allah Almighty sees him every second and that nothing is hidden from Him, not even what is in the heart. That explains the following tradition from Allah Almighty:

> *"O My slaves, if you think that I do not see you, there are defects in your faith. If you know that I see you, do not consider Me the least of those who observe you."*

This is the reality which all recognise but forget, or pretend to forget, in order to indulge the lower appetites of the self.

Allah Almighty says:

> *"He who created death and life to test which of you is best in action. He is Almighty, Ever-Forgiving."*
>
> (67:2)

When Allah Almighty speaks about the wisdom of creation and the fact that life is the arena of choice for us so that we can choose to obey Allah in the best manner, worship Him in the best manner, and cling to the Path of Allah in the best manner, He mentions death before mentioning life. He does so in order that this world may cease to deceive us. However much man is deluded and ascribes what is in existence to himself, Allah Almighty reminds him of death to inform him that all the blessing, dominion and everything in this world has an end and nothing will last forever. If a human being remembers that, then this world, which he must certainly leave, will not deceive him. Yet human delusion makes people imagine that they will live for years and years and believe that the time remaining to them is long.

The suddenness of death

Allah Almighty can make death occur without any apparent cause, and He can make it come suddenly at any moment. It is by no means certain that a man who enjoys good health will live for a long time or that a man who is young has a long life in front of him. Death comes to both young and old, healthy and sick. A man may die in the best of health or when very young, and a sick man may live until he reaches a great age.

Because Allah Almighty loves us He does not desire us to be deluded by life or to be confident that it will last a long time. We must expect the end at any time, so that we hasten to perform good deeds and refrain from acts of disobedience. If I knew for certain that I would die at the age of fifty or sixty, then I would commit acts of disobedience, wrong people and take unlawful wealth until I reached a year or two before my appointed term and then repent to Allah and do good. If this were to be the case the world would be full of acts of disobedience and there would be very little good. But when I know that my life could end at any moment, I hasten to do good. That is why Allah describes His righteous servants who have a high position, at the head of whom are the Prophets, as people of action.

"They outdid one another in good actions, calling out to Us in yearning and in awe." (21:9)

Outdoing one another in good actions is desirable because tomorrow is not guaranteed. This is part of the wisdom inherent in the concealment of the time of death. It makes us hasten to return to the Path of Allah before death surprises us at any moment, day or night.

To summarise this chapter, we say that all existence was created for man and it is subjected to him by the power of Allah, not through his own efforts. The knowledge which Allah has revealed to us is part of His laws in the earth, which have been in operation since the beginning of creation even though they were hidden from us. In this universe man does not even own himself. The Spirit which enters the body to give it life and whose departure makes it die, is the concern of Allah. None of us are acquainted with its secret. Since man does not own his own life in this existence, how can he own the rest of existence? As this world approaches its end, man feels that he has power over it and he uses the science which Allah has disclosed to him to combat and deny faith instead of using it to acknowledge the immensity and power of Allah.

Chapter Three
A Believer's Approach to Life

Allah Almighty wants us to approach life with faith in Him. We should realise that any scientific advance can only occur by the power of Allah, and should therefore increase our certainty in the existence of Allah. As a general rule, however, the opposite happens. As time passes we put our faith more and more in man's power and distance ourselves from Allah. Even though Allah Almighty has made it clear to us that all the events which occur in this universe pre-existed in His knowledge before they were actually brought about, there are still those who claim that clever human beings can produce things by their own power.

The consequence of this is that whenever there is a scientific advance which opens to us some new aspect of the laws of the universe, we suppose that we are the ones who have established the laws and that they act by our command, not by the power of the One who subjected them to us. We think that we are the ones who make things happen as we wish, and that we can achieve anything we want by our knowledge. But the truth is that man is powerless to accomplish anything in existence, for existence does not deviate from what Allah wishes to happen. There is nothing in existence which is outside of the command of Allah.

Some people say about those who reject and do not believe in Allah, "Did Allah Almighty will them to be unbelievers?" We say to such people that the unbelievers oppose the *Shari'a* which Allah designated for mankind but they are unable to oppose the actual control of Allah over existence. It is in their power to oppose the commands and prohibitions of the *Shari'a*, because

Allah created them with the choice to obey or disobey. If Allah Almighty had not given them this freedom of choice, none of them would have been able to disobey. So everything in existence is created in total subjugation except mankind and the jinn, who have freedom of choice where action is concerned.

We say to each and every one of those who claim to have unlimited choice in existence: "Just because you refuse to obey Allah in His Way and you reject it, do not suppose that you have unlimited free choice in existence. You are absolutely subject to Allah's decree. If that is not the case, then tell me if you are able to defend yourself against illness and can choose to be always healthy. You cannot. When death comes to you, reject the decree of Allah and say, 'I will not die!' You cannot. When you suffer an affliction in respect of your family or children, prevent it. You cannot. When your heart stops, make it start beating again. You cannot. That is because you are compelled in some things while you have choice in others. You have choice in certain matters because Allah so wishes. Do not let that choice delude you into thinking you are not absolutely subject to Allah's laws in existence."

Now that Allah has disclosed to man some of the secrets in existence which have enabled him to fly in the air, plumb the depths of the seas, travel to the moon, and bring near things which were once far away, man has begun to think that he has power over everything. We say to anyone who ignorantly claims this, "If you have power, as you claim, then your power over things should enable you to get everything you desire. The truth is that you are empowered by the command of Allah to make use of the laws of Allah in the earth, but you cannot make these laws conform to your desires. So what happens in existence is beyond the power of all mankind. Otherwise, why do events surprise people and why do those who own little not own a lot? And how is it that some of those who once ruled a people or a state become outcasts, and exiled in a single day, fleeing from place to place, hiding from people in a effort to prolong their lives?"

Allah, the only One who has judgement and command, is able to remove life, rulership, or property from a person in a single day or a single instant, even if he came to rule by his own choice and abilities in such a way that no one can wrest his position from him. For the truth is that his position only came about through the power of Allah and the means of Allah in existence. That is why Allah Almighty can at any moment remove from him what He gave him and make someone else succeed him. Read the words of Allah Almighty:

> *"Say, 'O Allah, Master of the Kingdom, You give sovereignty to whoever You will. You take sovereignty from whoever You will. You exalt whoever You will You abase whoever You will. All good is in Your hands. You have power over all things."* (3:26)

So sovereignty does not come to you by your own capacity and is not removed from you by Your own will. It is the decree of Allah Almighty that gives you sovereignty and removes sovereignty from you. When you respect the decree of Allah, He gives you what He wishes. If you are disobedient towards Him, He will take from you what He gives you. Allah Almighty says in a *Hadith Qudsi*:

> "O son of Adam, if you are pleased with what I have allotted to you, I will grant repose to your heart and body. If you are not pleased with what I have allotted to you, then by My might and majesty, I will give this world power over you so that you run in it as wild beasts run in the wilderness. You will only obtain from it what I have allotted you, and you will be blameworthy in My sight.

Allah Almighty grants man some strength from His strength, some wealth from His wealth, and some power from His power;

but man believes that he has this by his own abilities and that he may act in whatever way he wills. In the course of making improvements to his material standard of living, man has been able to achieve certain things and has made some discoveries, but all these discoveries did not take place out of nothing. People can only use the substances which Allah has created and the intellect Allah has given them in whatever they do.

Take the example of glass, for instance. Man uses a substance which already exists in the earth – a certain type of sand – and the energy which Allah created in the universe to produce this glass. There is, however, a difference between what human beings produce and that which is achieved by the power of Allah Almighty. Man cannot give life to any of the things he produces, nor can he make them multiply by themselves to produce others like them. The work of His creatures remains as it is and does not engender others like it. The workmanship of Allah Almighty, however, is of a different order. He creates out of nothing without need for something which already exists. So not only is the product created by Him but the matter itself of which it is composed is also created by Him. That is the difference between the workmanship of the Creator and the workmanship of the created beings.

Allah is the Best of Creators

That which Allah Almighty has produced grows by itself and reproduces others like it by a natural process of propagation. A creature cannot achieve that. Allah does not begrudge His creatures calling themselves "creators" but He has called Himself "the Best of Creators". Read the words of Allah:

"So blessed be Allah, the Best of Creators!" (23:14)

29

Allah Almighty creates from nothing, whereas You create from things that already exist. He creates what feels and grows but what you make has neither feeling nor growth. What He creates can multiply by itself, but you cannot do that. If you want food, for instance, you go to the earth, plough it and cultivate it and then harvest it, mill the grain, make bread and prepare food, thus taking from what has been created by Allah through the idea which He has given you and using the energy with which He has provided you. All these things are gifts from Allah. In all that I do I use something which already exists. I did not bring about the basic substance and matter of existence. That was created by Allah Almighty.

From where do you get the seeds you plant which produce a crop for you? From a previous harvest. From where did the previous harvest come? From one before that. You can take that back to the first seeds before there was any human intervention. They were the work of Allah, who does everything with perfection. The seeds come from Allah Almighty, Who brought them into existence out of nothing. It is the same with everything in existence. The first bringing into existence was done by Allah and He then guided man to recognise the special qualities of this original existence in order to utilise it and give it a second, third and fourth existence, and so on. Thus the cycle of life revolves again and again. Read the words of the Almighty:

"As We originated the first creation so We will regenerate it." (21:104)

Thus with certainty we arrive at the fact that the origin of everything in this world is from Allah Almighty. Perhaps you will now speak about hereditary traits and how it is possible to exploit that to improve species of plants and other things. Did you bring those hereditary traits into existence or are they part of the creation of Allah Almighty? You are still taking from something which already exists. If you really want to ascribe

30

creation to yourselves, then bring these hereditary traits into existence from nothing. If you do not – and you will not do so – then respect the creation of Allah in existence and ascribe everything to Allah, not to yourselves.

This is Allah's Creation

When man sees civilisation and progress, he must think as a believer and use his insight to see that it is Allah who has subjugated these existent things to him. Once I was visiting the city of San Francisco in America and people there wanted to dazzle me with what science has achieved. They took me to the largest hotel, in which everything was operated by buttons and service was carried out by automated means so that you obtained what you wanted without any need to leave your room. You pressed a button and the cup of coffee arrived. You pressed another button and there was a cup of tea or the food you wanted. They asked me what I thought of it all and I said, "If this is what man can achieve with his powers, just think what the Garden which was created by the power of Allah Almighty must be like. It contains delights many, many times greater than anything man can achieve – however great his technological advances might be."

Furthermore, the accomplishment of all this was preceded by human efforts in which a large number of people participated. There are people who grow and grind the coffee, who manufacture the sugar, who fill and oversee the machines so that they do not run out. So any benefit produced by human powers is not in fact as you experience it. It does not simply happen in an instant on the touch of a button: behind it there is a long process of preparation in which a large number of people have participated. So it is not really a question of pressing a button and the machine giving you what you want. That is just an appearance.

However much mankind progresses in science, it will never enable him to do what he wants merely by the idea occurring to his mind so that it materialises in front of him. That is impossible and absolutely inconceivable. But in Paradise, by the Power of Allah Almighty, if a thing merely comes to your mind you will find it in front of you. You will not find it in front of you by any human capacity, but by the power of Allah Almighty alone. That is the perspective which a believer should bring to every scientific advance.

We are told, for instance, that aeroplanes will develop to the point that we will be able to go right round the world in an hour. This has not yet happened, but if it does, then we will meet it with the words, "Glory be to Allah!" All of this scientific progress is merely the uncovering of the laws of Allah in the earth and making use of the means He has provided. But what bliss will we encounter when we move from laws of causation to the Power of the Causer?

This human progress should make it easier for our minds to discern the powers which Allah has placed in the universe so that we recognise the immensity of our Creator and realise that what we will encounter in the Next World, if Allah wills, will be indescribable bliss. These things should not distance us from faith but rather should bring us closer to it. These things should not deceive us about ourselves and our intellects but rather increase us in humility towards Allah Almighty. The problem is that we do not understand this knowledge in the light of faith but take it as showing that man has by his own power brought these things into existence.

When man reached the moon, what did people say in explanation of this noble *ayat*?

"O company of jinn and men! If you are able to pierce through the confines of the heavens and earth, pierce through them. You will not pierce through except with a clear authority." (55:33)

Some of them said that man had pierced through the confines of the heavens and earth despite the fact that Allah Almighty has challenged the jinn and men to do so. Some scientists, wanting to mitigate the matter for Allah Almighty, said that what is meant by this *ayat* is the authority of science. We say to them, "What is meant here is the authority of Allah Almighty. Do not try to mitigate it and do not undervalue the powers of Allah, the Almighty and Majestic."

The moon which they reached is in the vicinity of the earth and the closest celestial body to it. Where is the moon in relation to the unknowable vastness of the heavens? It is merely an earthbound satellite in the lowest heaven above which are the seven heavens, each heaven occupying an awesome expanse known only to its Creator. Allah Almighty says:

> *"We have adorned the lowest heaven with the beauty of the planets."* (37:6)

All that we can see from the earth is part of the lowest heaven, in which are stars which are countless millions of light years distant. If all of the energy that exists in the earth were combined, it would still not be able to send one human being into space at the speed of light, regardless of whether the human body would be able to bear this velocity or not. Even if we were to hypothesise that a man could travel at the speed of light, it would still require millions of years to reach those stars. This much we know. Yet there are still worlds and suns about which we know nothing at all.

Although human science has been able, by means of telescopes, to penetrate such immense distances into space, we still have no idea of the true size of the universe. So where is the moon in relation to that distance? The distance from the earth to the moon is virtually nothing in comparison to the size of the heavens whose extent no human being can reach — except by the authority of Allah Almighty.

But why does Allah say, "except with a clear authority," and not stop at *"O company of jinn and men! If you are able to pierce through the confines of the heavens and earth, pierce through them"*? The answer is that if the noble *ayat* were to stop at the inability of the jinn and men to pierce through the confines of the heavens and the earth, that would cause doubt about the miracle of the Night Journey and Ascent of the Messenger of Allah, may Allah bless him and grant him peace, through the seven heavens. The Messenger of Allah, may Allah bless him and grant him peace, alone of all of Allah's creatures – angels, jinn, men and others – went beyond the Lote-Tree of the Boundary. The Lote-Tree of the Boundary is the place at which the knowledge of every creature, even the angels close to Allah, stops – even by Revelation.

The words of the Almighty, *"You will not pierce through except with a clear authority,"* stress the truth of the miracle of the Ascent of the Prophet because the Messenger of Allah, may Allah bless him and grant him peace, reached the Lote-Tree of the Boundary and passed beyond it by the authority of Allah Almighty. Jibril preceded the Messenger of Allah, may Allah bless him and grant him peace, in the Night Journey and Ascent; and he ascended through one heaven after another until he reached the Lote-Tree of the Boundary.

Then Jibril stopped and asked the Messenger of Allah, may Allah bless him and grant him peace, to go ahead. Jibril said to our Messenger, peace and blessings be upon him, "If I were to go forward, I would be burned up. But if you go forward, Muhammad, you will pass beyond." All of this happened solely by the authority and power of Allah Almighty. Perhaps the formation of the body of the Messenger of Allah, may Allah bless him and grant him peace, was changing as he ascended from heaven to heaven to be able to bear that Divine light in the heavens.

We say to those who say that what is meant by this *ayat* is the authority of science, "Where is the authority of science in relation to the power of Allah Almighty?" Allah says in His precise *ayats*:

"You have only been given a little knowledge." (17:85)

Is this little knowledge the authority by which man will pierce through the confines of the heavens and the earth? Of course not. That is why all of those who say that this refers to the authority of science overstep in their explanation. It is the authority of Allah alone which allowed our Prophet, may Allah bless him and grant him peace, to ascend to the Lote-Tree of the Boundary and pass beyond it.

Faith and scientific progress

I say to those who are deluded by human science that it is the small amount of knowledge given by Allah to man that has produced all of the civilisations and scientific progress which we see and which the coming generations after us will see until the Day of Rising. If this small amount of knowledge that has produced all of this, what is the knowledge of Allah capable of producing for us in the Next World? Scientific progress should increase our belief in Allah and fear of Him while we live in the world of material causes.

In this world human beings vary in their capacity to respond to the means Allah has given us. The hand of Allah offers those means to all His creatures, and a person who takes and uses these means with vigour is stronger than someone else who does not. A portion of the earth which a human being cares for, cultivates well and sows with good seeds gives him a good crop. But if one leaves the earth without tillage or cultivation, it will not give him anything. This is the gift of the Lord.

Allah has created in existence things which act "for you" and things which act "by you". Things which act for you give you a return without any effort or action on your part. They are a gift for which you do not have to work. The sun, moon, stars, and atmosphere all give to you without you having to exert any effort or any action of any sort. They are given equally to all, and not to one person more than another. They are not singled out for specific people or groups of people to the exclusion of others. These are things which act for you.

As for the things which act by you, this description applies to many things on the earth. If you till and sow, the earth will give you its fruit. If you do not till and do not sow, it will not give you anything. If you dig in the earth you will find petrol, minerals and other things which are inside it. If you do not dig, the earth will not give you any of its treasures.

Increase in living standards and the disparity between different nations come from the things which act by you. Whoever works with effort and earnestness progresses in utilising the means at their disposal and advances among nations. Whoever does not work does not receive anything. It is more proper for us, as a nation of believers who have understand the gifts of Allah, to make use of the means the earth gives us to advance in the gifts we have been given. But we fail to do so: we leave others to advance by utilising the means common to all of us while we do nothing. Allah Almighty gives progress in this world to nations who make use of means, even if they are unbelievers.

"If anyone desires to cultivate the Next World, We will increase him in his cultivation. If anyone desires to cultivate this world, We will give him some of it; but he will have no share in the Next World." (42:20)

The gift of this world is the gift of the Lord which we must take by the means He has given us. Allah Almighty gave us the components necessary for life and its continuance, at the beginning of creation and without our having to do anything to acquire them. From the time of Adam, water, air and food – which are the necessities of life – have been guaranteed for man because Allah Almighty is the One who called him into existence and therefore He ensures that he has the basic constituents of his life.

Allah brought into existence the water which we drink, the food which we eat, the air which we breathe and the earth on which we live. All of these are necessities of life which have existed for man from the beginning of his existence on the earth without him having to expend any effort to bring them about.

But if I want my life to be more luxurious and to elevate it then I must employ my intellect, which was created by Allah to adapt the universe which Allah created and subjugated to me. By that means I will reach a more comfortable life which means, as we said above, that things are accomplished in a shorter time and with less effort.

The Signs of Allah and progress

Allah Almighty has given us the necessities of life. He has given us our intellect and the means by which we can provide ourselves with the luxuries of life. Then He asks us to reflect on His Signs in existence. We continually see these Signs but are heedless of them. All the progress which has taken place has come about through scientists, who have reflected on the phenomena of existence and have thus been able to discover the laws of Allah in existence and use them to achieve scientific advances. This is what science is – grasping and taking advantage of the Signs of Allah in the earth.

But did Allah Almighty create us simply to live in the world of means? No, this is merely one stage of the long journey of life. In the stage during which we live in this world of means we must toil so that later we can rest. Those who have discovered all the inventions by which mankind has benefited, toiled until they were successful in them. Sometimes they spent many long sleepless nights in their search. They strove until they achieved what they desired. That is the law of this world: you must study in order to pass your exams, you must work to obtain a salary, and so forth.

Allah Almighty desired to call our attention to the fact that there is another gift greater than all these temporal gifts – the gift of recognising Allah as God. In order to deserve this, the greatest gift of Allah, you must be serious and perform righteous actions in this world and cling to the Path of Allah until you find rest in the bliss bestowed by Allah in the Next World. However hard you work in this world and whatever worldly blessings you enjoy, the inevitable end is that you will lose them when you die. But in the Next World Allah Almighty will make bliss eternal if you exhausted yourself following His Way in this world.

To summarise, the Path of belief demands that whenever man increases in knowledge, he must also increase in belief in Allah and fear of Him. We must ascribe everything in existence to its Creator, the One who brought it into existence: that is Allah, glory be to Him and Exalted is He! We know that it would not be possible for us to advance or to increase our comforts in life unless Allah Almighty had placed in existence secrets and laws which enable us to do so. But instead of ascribing things to the One who really brought them about, we ascribe them to ourselves and believe that we have achieved them on our own and through our own knowledge. We imagine that we control things by our intellects and our laws, not that it is Allah who has subjected those things to us. This is deviating far from the Path of Allah. Man has deceived himself by his intellect into believing that he has power over the universe. True happiness can only come from recognising Allah and submitting to Him.

Chapter Four
The Familiar will come to an End

Human beings live in this world and we become accustomed to the things we are used to seeing and living with, to the point that they become taken for granted and we do not pay any attention to them. That is what we call the immutable and unchanging aspect of the life of this world. We are used to seeing the sun rise and set every day. We are used to the alternation of night and day. We are used to the seas with their continual movement and the land with its firm, unchanging appearance. We have become used to the gift of all the constant things in existence, which is why we do not think about them. We take them for granted as if they were an inalienable right. We do not reflect on their creation or their organisation, or about the Strength and Power which created them and preserves them and makes them continue to work in such a precise and fine way. Most people do not think about the unchanging gifts of existence. They take them as if they thought they were self-sustaining and gave themselves to them of their own accord.

It is truly extraordinary that people increase in knowledge as time progresses but at the same time decrease in adhering to the Way of Allah. Every day our knowledge of the laws and Signs of Allah in existence increases, and so it might be supposed that such knowledge would bring us nearer to Allah Almighty because it discloses to us some of the secrets of the power of Allah in the universe. But the increase in knowledge results in an increase in our appetites in respect of the life of this world and our attachment to it and our materialistic ideas about it. The more time passes, the more appetite dominates the human soul. That confirms the words of the Almighty:

"No indeed! Truly man is unbridled, seeing himself as self-sufficient. Truly the return is to your Lord." (96:6-8)

Human oppression and tyranny raise their head whenever we think that we are self-sufficient and have no need of Allah Almighty or to worship. Science appears to achieve for us what we desire. When we want to travel we find comfortable, easy and quick routes in air-conditioned aeroplanes which preclude excessive fatigue. When we want food and drink we find it prepared for us by modern means and in sterile containers. While sitting in your room you can watch the television and see anything you want anywhere in the world. If you become ill you can find the most modern scientific equipment which sees and analyses everything inside your body and shows us where the illness is, what it is and the method to treat it.

Modern equipment shows us X-rays of everything in the human body. CAT scans of the brain show us any blood clots or injury that is there. Liver scans define for us where the illness is, how severe it is and how to treat it. Blood analysis has advanced to give us an exact picture of all the constituents of blood. The result of this is that people believe that it is the doctor who heals. But the doctor only treats: Allah is the One who heals.

The treatment may be incorrect and become a means of hastening our end. Cure may come at the hands of a young, newly graduated, doctor after the failure of his professors who taught him to diagnose illnesses. That does not mean that this young doctor knows more than his teachers from whom he took his knowledge. It simply means that every healing has a time decreed by Allah Almighty. When the ordained time for healing comes, Allah reveals to the junior doctor the secret of the cure, while his professors were unable to find it because the time had not yet come. Yet people do not pay any attention to this. They rather ascribe healing to the genius of the doctor!

People rarely remember that only Divine Power is effective. They rely more and more on human power and what it can apparently achieve. They turn to the secondary causes and forget the Causer. They esteem the blessing and forget the Blesser. When one of them is presented with a variety of excellent fruit, he says, "This has been produced by such-and-such a farmer." They forget the Giver and the Creator of this, who is Allah – glory be to Him and Exalted is He!

Few of us, unfortunately, when we take food, begin with "In the Name of Allah who gives, creates and bestows". When they are full, few people say, "Praise be to Allah" to Him who provided them with those blessings they have enjoyed. Man exalts his intellect and believes that the blessings he achieves in life are the result of his intellect. He thinks he has them because he is intelligent and uses his intelligence, and prides himself on that in front of people. He believes that the blessings will continue because he has managed his life well and attended to everything. He resembles the owner of the two gardens in the Qur'an who ascribed the blessings of them to himself, and whose words to himself are reported in the Qur'an:

> "He entered his garden, wronging himself, and said, 'I do not think that this will ever end. I do not think the Hour will ever come. But if I should be sent back to my Lord, I will definitely get something better in return.'" (18:35-36)

It is as if the owner of the two gardens ascribed his blessings to himself and said that he was able to preserve them by purely human means and make them endure indefinitely, and that they would never be taken away from him. How wrong he was! When we see something beautiful, we should praise its Maker, but these days we praise mankind and say, "So-and-so has turned his land into a paradise! So-and-so has done this and that! This is due to so-and-so's industry!" We do not say "by the help of Allah" or "success is from Allah". We fail to remember Allah Almighty, who is the Giver and the Withholder!

Following the Law and the protection of society

We habitually rely on things which make life easier and more comfortable for us. We think that we sustain ourselves through our work independently of the power of Allah. Man believes in himself to the extent that he legislates laws for himself which are contrary to the Way of Allah. He does not stop there but goes on to describe the divinely revealed Path as being too arduous – or says that it is backward or not suitable for our time. The truth is that it is the person who puts himself far from the Way of Allah who is backward.

The underlying reason for man's arrogance and reliance on his material life is that this materialism does not limit us to a particular way of behaving which restricts our appetites, whereas the Path of Way puts limits on our behaviour in life in a way which will ensure respect and honour for us, yet we pay no attention to that. For when Allah Almighty tells me not to steal, He is not merely limiting my freedom to put my hands on other people's property: that is a narrow view. What He is in fact doing is restraining the rest of society from putting their hands on my property. So He protects me, the weak individual, from society which could easily strip me of everything.

When Allah Almighty asks me not to violate someone else's honour, He does, of course, limit my freedom so that if I am attracted to a woman who is married to someone else I do not seduce her or violate her. But I should also notice that by prescribing this law Allah Almighty has also forbidden thousands of other husbands and young men from violating my honour. This is what the Law of Allah does: it protects me and protects my property, honour and children. But my narrow view and immediate appetites make me forget what Allah is protecting me from and resent being restricted in any way. This is why however much material civilisation advances human behaviour declines and deteriorates. What was unlawful becomes allowed by the custom of society, not by the laws of Allah.

But whenever man thinks that he is self-sufficient because of his knowledge, rank, wealth, strength or anything else which Allah has given him, Allah Almighty comes and disabuses him of that idea and shows him the truth. That happens through death or the arrival of the Last Hour and the destruction of everything familiar to man in this world which he believes he has achieved by himself. So Allah Almighty tells him, "If you achieved it by yourself, then preserve it if you have any means of doing so."

The first truth in life is death and when faced with death everyone in this world stops powerless, humble and abased. The most famous doctors, whom others believe can preserve their health for them and prolong their lives, stand humble and powerless before death. They have no devices and can do nothing to keep it from themselves. The same applies to all the material blessings which man believes he can have as he likes and however he wants. They also inevitably come to an end.

At the moment of death, the human being sees clearly visible before him things which were previously hidden from him but about which Allah informed him and asked him to believe in. It is the moment when mankind is totally dumbfounded. The human being, who had believed that he was strong, powerful and mighty, becomes humble and fearful, powerless to do anything.

When the spirit leaves the body, man leaves all he is familiar with in this world for another world in which nothing is familiar to him. Death is not the end, as many people believe, but a transition from one form of life to another, from the life of this world, which has its laws, to an interspatial life, which has other laws. One sees things he was not previously able see. That is why Allah Almighty says:

> "So We have stripped you of your covering and today your sight is sharp." (50:22)

The Messenger of Allah, may Allah bless him and grant him peace said in a noble *hadith*:

43

"People are asleep and when they die, they wake up."

How can the Messenger of Allah, may Allah bless him and grant him peace, say, "People are asleep and when they die, they wake up"? How can the Messenger of Allah, may Allah bless him and grant him peace say, "People are asleep" when they are awake in the life in which they live, and "When they die, they wake up"? How can it be that man, who is awake and alive, filling the earth with movement, is asleep, but then when he dies and is lying lifeless in his grave he wakes up?

We reply that in the life of this world people are distracted by their appetites and property and what they desire to achieve in it. All those things distract them from the reality of the life of this world, so that they do not reflect on the Signs of Allah. Even though Allah Almighty sends them proof after proof to induce them to believe they still turn away. It is as though they were asleep to the reality of what is around them. When they die, they see everything that Allah promised them in a manifest way and with absolute clarity.

The sleeping man proceeds without guidance because his eyes are closed to the truth. When he opens his eyes, he sees and knows for certain. Then the first thing which severs man from what he is familiar with is death. When one is dying he sees that his destination is either Paradise or Hell. At the moment of death one knows for certain that he is dying because of what he sees at that time. People believe that dying is the same for every-one – a human is on the point of death and then dies. But the truth is that Allah Almighty tells us that at the moment of death, when people depart from this world they do not all depart in the same manner. The difference begins here. Read the words of the Almighty:

> "That is how Allah repays the godfearing, those the angels take in a virtuous state, saying, 'Peace be upon you! Enter the Garden for what you did.'" (16:31-32)

When a virtuous believer dies he sees the angels. The unbeliever who has no faith also sees angels while he is dying – but angels of a completely different, and indeed terrifying, form. The virtuous believer sees angels of mercy who come to him bringing good news of the Garden and greeting him with peace and with their happy beautiful faces. Then the believer is happy because he is being transported to a good life which is better than the one he had in this world. His face is smiling and his features are joyful. He sees that the abode of testing has come to an end and that he is being transported to the Abode of Bliss, in which things happen directly by the power of Allah Almighty. His face is radiant. When you look at someone dying in this way, you recognise that he senses that he is moving to a better place than the place he was living and that Allah's promise to him of a good outcome has actually been realised.

The unbeliever will also see angels when he is dying. Allah Almighty describes this woeful encounter:

> *"If only you could see when the angels take back the believers at their death, beating their faces and their backs: 'Taste the punishment of the Burning! That is for what you did. Allah does not wrong His slaves.'"*
>
> (8:50-51)

Thus we see the awesome difference between the believer and the unbeliever at the moment of death. The angels say to the unbeliever: "Come, now you will see what you used to deny in the world. You will see the punishment which awaits you. If you have any power or strength, then get yourselves out of this! Flee if you can – but you cannot. Your power in this world deluded you, so you transgressed, wronged others and disobeyed Allah. You said things about Allah which were not true. You were arrogant on the earth. Now all that you were familiar with in life in the lower world has come to an end. The deities you worshipped rather than Allah have fled and hidden themselves because they are false. Your friends who used to abet you in falsehood and disobedience to Allah have no power now to help you or even themselves. All those who helped you in this world without right are now unable to protect you."

Exposure to Hellfire

The Noble Qur'an tells us that at the moment of death the angels will beat and hurt unbelievers who denied the blessings of Allah and refused to thank Him for them. It is known that punishment can only take place when there is life; you cannot punish a dead body. In order for the body to feel the punishment, there must be life in it. That is why when the angels strike and inflict injury, it takes place at the moment of death while there is still life in the body. That is why at the moment of death you will find the faces of the unbelievers gloomy and their muscles and faces contracted: they see the evil destination which awaits them.

At the moment of death, therefore, the believer and unbeliever are differentiated, which does not apply in this world. In this world an unbeliever may have rank, might, authority, and nobility which a believer may not have. But at the moment of death the separation begins. All that we were familiar with in the life of this world comes to an end when the unbeliever sees the angels bringing the beginnings of the punishment and they rain down blows on him. The believer sees the angels bringing him the beginnings of bliss and the good news of the Garden. Indeed, there is a challenge issued by the angels to the unbeliever at the moment of death. Read the words of Allah:

"If you could only see the wrongdoers in the throes of death when the angels are stretching out their hands: 'Disgorge your own selves! Today you will be repaid with the punishment of humiliation for saying other than the truth about Allah, and being arrogant about His Signs.'"

(6:93)

The angels say to every dying wrongdoer or unbeliever, "If you have power, as you used to claim in this world, then extricate yourself from this situation. Save yourself if you have power or effective authority, but you will not be able to do so. In the life of this world you claimed that you had strength and power, but now you know the truth. You know that all strength and power belong to Allah alone and that whatever capacity, strength or authority you did have in reality belonged to Allah. You yourself possess nothing. It appeared to you that you had capability and strength and that you had power, but now you are in the moment of truth in which there is no supposition or doubt. Now you know for certain that it was self-delusion."

After dying, then, people move to the life of the Interspace (*barzakh*), which is the dimension they inhabit during the period between their death and the Resurrection. Allah Almighty has informed us a little about the laws which apply there. A human being can hear when he is dead but cannot reply. The Messenger of Allah, may Allah bless him and grant him peace, spoke to the dead unbelievers after the Battle of Badr and called out to them, "Abu Jahl ibn Hisham! Umayya ibn Khalaf! 'Utba ibn Rabi'a! Shayba ibn Rabi'a! Have you found what your Lord promised you to be true? I have found what my Lord promised me to be true." 'Umar, may Allah be pleased with him, heard what the Messenger of Allah, may Allah bless him and grant him peace, said and asked, "Messenger of Allah, how can they hear and answer when they are corpses?" He said, "By Him who has my soul in His hand, they hear what I say to them, but they cannot reply."

Allah Almighty informs us in the Noble Qur'an about some of what will happen to the dead in their graves. He says:

"The Fire, to which, morning and night, they are exposed and, on the Day the Hour takes place: 'Admit Pharaoh's people to the harshest punishment!'" (40:46)

47

That means that there is some form of life in the Interspace between this world and the Next and that it is a type of life in which the human being is conscious and can discriminate between things. If people in the grave were still and silent and completely dead to existence, it would not be possible for the people of Pharaoh to be exposed to the Fire twice every day. The fact that they are exposed to the Fire means that they are able to discriminate. If that were not so, they would not be able to recognise that it was a Fire and that they were going to be punished in it; and their being exposed to the Fire every day would be completely meaningless. But the truth is that they experience intense pain because they know for certain that they are heading for terrible punishment. Expectation of affliction is sometimes worse than its actual occurrence.

Time – and life in the Interspace (*Barzakh*)

The words of Allah Almighty, *"The Fire, to which, morning and night, they are exposed,"* indicate that there is a sort of time in life in the Interspace because morning and night are attributes of time. But when are Pharaoh's people exposed to the fire morning and night? This noble *ayat* describes for us two states of the people of Pharaoh: being exposed to the Fire and entering the Fire. Were Pharaoh's people exposed to the Fire in the life of this world? No, because if they had been exposed to the Fire while they were still in the life of this world, they would have prostrated to Allah Almighty and slain the false god Pharaoh because he was leading them to Hell. This is in accordance with the words of Allah Almighty:

"He will go ahead of his people on the Day of Rising and lead them down into the Fire. What an evil watering-hole to be led to!" (11:98)

If the people of Pharaoh had been shown the Fire in this world, they would have known that their worship of Pharaoh would lead them to the punishment and they would never have worshipped him. If we were to say that the Pharaoh's people are shown the Fire on the Day of Rising, that would be an error, for on the Day of Rising they will enter it. Allah Almighty says:

"And, on the Day the Hour takes place: 'Admit Pharaoh's people to the harshest punishment!'" (40:46)

So there are three stages in the life of the human being: life in this world; between death and the Resurrection (which is the life of the Interspace); and life after the Final Hour comes. We will try to define where in these three stages Pharaoh's people are exposed to the Fire. If it did not happen in this world and if on the Day of Rising they will enter the Fire then the exposure referred to must take place between death and the resurrection, in the life of the Interspace.

So there is life in the Interspace and it is during this interspatial life that the people of Pharaoh are exposed to the Fire. Are they exposed to the Fire while they are in their graves or does that occur by Allah Almighty gathering them elsewhere to be exposed to the Fire? Whether that exposure takes place in their graves or by some other means, we know from the noble *ayat* that there is a type of life in the Interspace in which there is consciousness and feeling. We also know that in the Interspace man knows whether his final destination will be Paradise or Hell, and that he will see his place in the Garden or his place in the Fire. That is confirmed by the Messenger of Allah, may Allah bless him and grant him peace, who said:

"The grave is either one of the meadows of the Garden or one of the pits of the Fire."

That is why punishment in the grave, when a person sees his place in the Fire, is a dreadful punishment because, as we said, expectation of affliction can be worse than its occurrence. For instance, if you were to know for certain that your only son was going to die in a car accident in a year's time, would that not be a terrible torment for you throughout that year? It could be so painful that you would actually wish for the death to take place sooner so as to be spared torment. So the expectation of affliction is worse than its actual occurrence. There is another *ayat* about that in which Allah Almighty says:

> *"O you who believe! Do not make friends of people with whom Allah is angry, who have despaired of the Next World in the same way that the unbelievers have despaired of the inhabitants of the graves."* (60:13)

Let us look at the words of Allah Almighty, *"in the same way that the unbelievers have despaired of the inhabitants of the graves."* This means that the fact that they despair of there being any sort of consciousness in the graves is what has caused them to despair. But the fact that they despair also indicates that they know that their destination is the Fire.

These are some of the images which Allah gives us of the life of the Interspace so that we know that it is a kind of life which has its own laws. We know that Allah Almighty has singled out the people of Pharaoh to be exposed to the Fire during their life in the Interspace because of their arrogant tyranny and worship of Pharaoh. This is because they did not simply disobey commands but disobeyed the One who issues the commands. It is also because Musa brought the people of Pharaoh many Signs to confirm that Allah alone is Divine, but they mocked them.

The unbelievers and rebels will only enter Hell at the end of the Final Reckoning on the Day of Rising, but in the grave the human being will know his fate. Either he is blessed in his grave and is in bliss because he knows what awaits him, or he is one of the people of the Fire – we seek refuge with Allah – and he is suffering terrible torment because he knows what awaits him.

But the actual entry into the Garden or the Fire only takes place after the Reckoning on the Day of Rising.

To summarise, the more progress man achieves in science, the more he falsely supposes that he has power, that the power comes from himself, and that he is firmly established on the earth. Then death will come to awaken him from his great delusion, and he will realise that he has no intrinsic reality and that all that exists in this world has been produced by Allah - glory be to Allah and exalted is He! But the moment in which he could have repented has already passed because repentance at the moment of death is a forced repentance after one sees what he sees. Once people see their fate at the moment of death, repentance does not constitute an act of faith because faith must be in something unseen. As Allah Almighty says:

"Those who believe in the Unseen and establish the prayer."
(2:3)

Now what was unseen has been disclosed to him and the stage in which having faith is possible has come to an end.

Chapter Five
The Immutable changes

Allah Almighty has informed us that there is a form of life in the Interspace but some people believe that this life will resemble life as we know it in this world. This is an error because life in this world, life in the Interspace, and life in the Next World each have their own laws. All of these laws are completely different in respect of man's experience of them. Life in the Next World, for instance, is without end and there is no death in it, whereas there is death in this life. In the interspatial life that which was invisible to us is disclosed.

Allah Almighty has acquainted us with some of the Great Signs which will occur at the end of the world. We know with certainty that these Signs which we are discussing will be manifested, because Allah Almighty has informed us about them in His Book and through His Messenger; but it cannot be presumed that we know exactly how they will occur. There is a difference between believing in their reality and knowing how they will occur. How they will occur is part of the Unseen which is known by Allah Almighty alone. That is why Ibrahim asked his Lord how the process of bringing the dead to life will take place, as the Noble Qur'an tells us:

"When Ibrahim said, 'My Lord, show me how You bring the dead to life,' He asked, 'Do you not then believe?' He replied, 'Indeed I do! But so that my heart may be at peace.'" (2:260)

Some sceptics have tried to explain this *ayat* as indicating a deficiency in the faith of Ibrahim, the father of the Prophets, peace be upon him. This is a calumny against Ibrahim, because Allah Almighty made Ibrahim a model for all mankind. He purified him and subjected him to countless afflictions and tests in which he was as firm as the unmoving mountains. Allah also placed the major line of Prophethood among his descendants. All these honours could not have been given to Ibrahim, peace be upon him, if he had not been a believer in the most complete sense.

One of the fundamentals of faith is that Allah has the power to bring the dead to life, and Ibrahim was only asking how that takes place. Allah Almighty wanted Ibrahim and all people to understand that they should not ask "How?" where the power of Allah is concerned. You cannot ask "How?" where Allah Almighty is concerned. Allah says to anything, "Be!" and it is. How this takes place is beyond the power of any mind to understand. That is why Allah Almighty provided Ibrahim with an experiment:

"He said, 'Take four birds and train them to yourself. Then put a part of them on each mountain and call them. They will come rushing to you. Know that Allah is Mighty, Wise.'"

(2:260)

Did Allah Almighty tell Ibrahim, peace be upon him, how? No, but He enabled him to witness the event without telling him the secret because that, as we have already said, is beyond the capacity of the human intellect.

The test of believing in the Resurrection

This did not only happen in the case of Ibrahim. It also happened with one of the Jewish Prophets, Zakariyya, and also with Maryam, peace be upon her. Another of the Prophets of Israel passed by a town which had been destroyed by a punishment from Allah Almighty. The Noble Qur'an tells us what he said:

> *"Or the one who passed by a town which had fallen into ruin. He asked, 'How can Allah restore this to life when it has died?' Allah caused him to die for a hundred years, then brought him back to life."* (2:259)

This Prophet asked how Allah could restore a town to life after it had been completely destroyed. Allah wanted to call his attention to the fact that there is no "How?" with Allah, so He made him die for a hundred years and then resurrected him. The Qur'an reports to us the question asked of him:

> *"Then He asked, 'How long have you been here?' He replied, 'I have been here a day or part of a day.' He said, 'Not so! You have been here a hundred years.'"* (2:259)

When he asked "How?", Allah made him die a hundred years and then resurrected him. When he woke up, nothing in him had changed. He was in the same state as he was in when he died. He woke up as a strong young man with nothing around him to tell him that he had been dead for a hundred years. That is why when Allah Almighty asked him, "How long have you been here?" he made an analogy with a man's ordinary sleep and replied, "I have been here a day or part of a day." People do not sleep longer than that. Then Allah Almighty provided him with material evidence that he had been dead for a hundred years before being resurrected. Allah says:

> *"Look at your food and drink − it has not gone bad − and look at your donkey. Thus We can make you a Sign for all mankind. Look at the bones − how We raise them up and clothe them in flesh."* (2:259)

That is how Allah Almighty made that Prophet see how, by His power, He had preserved for him his food which had not been altered or changed by the passage of years. But when he looked at his donkey he found that it had died and decayed and dissolved until it was a rotting skeleton. That cannot happen in just a day. Then Allah Almighty provided him with yet another sign and let him witness the re-clothing of the bare bones, the restoration of life to his donkey. Then that Prophet said:

> *"Now I know that Allah has power over everything."*
> (2:259)

The release of the power of Allah Almighty caused time to stop as regards the food, so that it remained fresh and uncorrupted. But time continued to pass for the donkey and it turned into a skeleton. In His unrestricted power, Allah Almighty can do a thing and its opposite simultaneously. But did Allah Almighty show him how that was achieved? No: the Almighty made him experience an actual instance of it so that he would know that Allah has power over everything.

When Zakariyya, peace be upon him, entered the *Mihrab* to visit Maryam, he found that she had fruit outside its normal season. What he did do? He turned to Allah Almighty by the proofs of His power which he could see before him, and asked Him to provide him with a son. But then Zakariyya remembered the secondary causes and how they were lacking in the case of both him and his wife. He said, as the Qur'an tells us:

> *"He said, 'O Lord, how can I possibly have a son when I have reached old age and my wife is barren?' He said, 'It shall be so. Allah does whatever He wills.'"* (3:40)

55

Secondary causes and Divine power

Did Allah Almighty explain to his Messenger Zakariyya how He would give him a son without recourse to the normal means? Normal circumstances would decree that his wife should not be barren and should not have reached an age at which women can no longer bear children. Furthermore, it would require that her husband was not a very old man, for whom it is generally impossible to father children. Thus, according to normal human conditions, Zakariyya's request was an impossible one. But the One who made the causes is not hampered by lack of secondary causes – His power is not limited or restricted by anything. Allah Almighty did not tell His Messenger how He would achieve it, but He said to him, *"It will be so. Allah does whatever He wills."*

When the angels gave Maryam, the daughter of 'Imran the good news that she would give birth to 'Isa, she was incredulous. Maryam had seen many miracles which broke the normal laws of cause and effect, as when Allah gave her food outside its normal season which appeared with her without anyone bringing it to her. That was a gift from Allah to her outside of normal means. But when she was given the good news of a son she reverted to dependence on secondary causes, as the Qur'an tells us:

> *"She said, 'How can I have a boy when no man has touched me and I am not an unchaste woman?' He said, 'It will be so! Your Lord says, "That is easy for Me; so that We may make him a Sign for mankind and a mercy from Us." It is a matter already decreed.'"* (19:20-21)

And in *Surat Al 'Imran:*

> *"She said, 'My Lord! How can I have a son when no man has ever touched me?' He said, 'It shall be so.' Allah creates*

56

whatever He wills. When He decides on something, He just says to it, 'Be!' and it is." (3:47)

So when Maryam asked how Allah would provide her with a son when no man had touched her – for in normal conditions in this world a child only results from the joining of a man and a woman – Allah Almighty did not tell her how that would be achieved. He said, *"It shall be so. Your Lord says..."*

This is what we see when the question "How?" is posed by the Prophets and Messengers whom Allah Almighty chose and selected from among His creatures and charged with conveying the Path of Heaven to the earth. With regard to how He brings about all that occurs, Allah Almighty says, *"It shall be so. Your Lord says..."*

The same applies when we discuss the Signs which Allah will show His slaves when the Hour is approaching its appointed time. We do not ask how they will occur, once we have seen the nature of Allah's power and know that Allah Almighty does not lack the power to do anything He wants in heaven or earth. Allah Almighty says in the Noble Qur'an, when informing us about the Signs which will occur as the End of Time approaches to proclaim the annihilation of the universe:

"When the Word is justly carried out against them, We will produce a Beast from the earth which will speak to them: 'Truly mankind had no certainty about Our Signs.'"

(27:82)

Allah Almighty informs us that after people have reached the pinnacle of worldly knowledge and science and think that they have everything under control and have mastery over all things, Allah Almighty will bring a Sign to demonstrate their powerlessness to them in the face of the overwhelming power of Allah Almighty.

Man has reached the moon and Mars. Every day science brings us something new. Science has eliminated distance, so that if something takes place in one place, people all over the world can see it at the very moment it takes place. A person can speak in any place in the world and his voice can be heard throughout the world at the very moment he is speaking. Inventions are coming which may achieve even more than that.

But during this time when man is being deluded by his knowledge and beguiled by what he has achieved, Allah Almighty will bring forth a Beast from the earth. This Beast will defy the powers of man. All the knowledge he has been granted and all the secrets of the universe that Allah has disclosed to man have not enabled him to make a beast speak; but Allah will bring forth to them from a earth a Beast which can speak.

But will this animal speak in one language alone – or will it speak all the languages of the earth so that the miracle will be greater? No one can say anything definitive, but what is sure is this beast will prove to all mankind that their knowledge is limited and restricted. Because of what they had achieved by their knowledge they believed that they had control of everything on earth. Then in the face of that false belief, they will find this Beast which speaks defying their knowledge and confirming their powerlessness.

This beast will be just one of the Signs indicating the approach of the Hour. We were told about another of the Signs of the Resurrection by the Messenger of Allah, may Allah bless him and grant him peace, when he said, "The Hour will not come until the sun rises from the west." People are used to the sun rising from the east. This familiar pattern happens by the Will of Allah Almighty who, at the end of time will turn it on its head for us and break the normal pattern.

We are not required to know how this will take place. The important thing is that the normal pattern of existence will be overturned and that Allah Almighty will take the immutable order to which all are accustomed and change it although man thought it would continue and remain the same forever without changing or altering, and that their science which they had acquired would give them strength and invincibility. A Sign of

Allah will undo all this in a single instant and people's power-lessness and incapacity will become clear to them. None of their strength or force will be of any avail to them in the face of the power of Allah Almighty.

When the Sun rises from the West

There is a difference, as we have said, between believing in a reality and knowing how this reality will take place. The Messenger of Allah, may Allah bless him and grant him peace, informed us that before the Last Hour comes, the sun will rise from the west. That reinforces for us the fact that Allah Almighty alone is the One who causes changes and is not sub-ject to change. Nothing in existence has immutability or perma-nence, and there will come a moment when Allah will change all that we see as stable. To make this easier to understand, let us take the solar system in which we live. What do we see? The earth revolves around the sun and the earth revolves on its axis. The moon revolves around the earth. Allah Almighty tells us in the Noble Qur'an:

> *"And the sun runs to its resting place. That is the decree of the Almighty, the All-Knowing."* (36:38)

Allah Almighty wanted to give us an indication of the move-ment of the sun, and so He says "runs" to convey to us that the movement of the sun is swift: running is quicker than walking. The "resting place" of the sun is a place which only Allah Almighty knows. As long as the sun is running to its resting place and all of its action has an equally strong reaction and opposite direction, we can imagine – and this is merely an attempt to make the image more comprehensible and has no connection whatsoever with how the event will actually take place – that it is possible that the resting place of the sun is the end of its movement in a certain direction and that it will reverse its course and rise from the west. The act of stopping at the resting place may cause it to reverse its direction so that then if it previously came from the east, it will now come from the west.

This is merely an attempt to make the idea easier to grasp, since none of us can be sure or even state with probability how it will take place. It is merely an approximate image to enable the human intellect to imagine how the sun could rise from the west. But we must not overlook an important fact relating to this great Sign, which is that once the sun rises from the west, repentance will not be accepted. The Messenger of Allah, may Allah bless him and grant him peace, said:

"Allah stretches forth His hand in the night to anyone who repents of evil done in the day, and He stretches forth His hand in the day to anyone who repents of evil done in the night – until the sun rises from the west."

So the rising of the sun from the west is one of the great Signs of Allah which will take place. Once it happens, then repentance will no longer be accepted.

Heaven and the Smoke

We move on to another Sign of the approach of the Last Hour. Read the words of the Almighty:

"So be on the watch for a day when heaven brings forth a distinctive smoke, enshrouding mankind. 'This is a painful punishment!' 'Our Lord, remove the punishment from us. We are truly believers.'" (44:10-12)

This is another of the great Signs of the end of the world. Heaven will produce a smoke which will cover all of the earth. This smoke will encompass every place after mankind has disobeyed Allah, become self-deluded and abandoned the Path of Allah, and believes that this world acts according to man-made laws. Then this smoke, which contains a punishment for mankind will come and envelop the earth. People will entreat Allah Almighty to remove the punishment from them because they now believe and promise to return to the Path of Allah. But as soon as Allah removes the punishment from them, they will revert to being unbelievers. Then after that the Great Blow and Divine Vengeance will overtake those who saw the Signs of Allah and denied them.

These phenomena which Allah Almighty reports to us and which His Messenger, may Allah bless him and grant him peace, conveyed, are the great Signs of the approach of the end of the world. Allah Almighty challenged all mankind to emulate His action and power, saying:

> *"O mankind! An example has been made, so listen to it carefully. Those whom you call upon besides Allah are not even able to create a single fly, even if they were to join together to do it. And if a fly steals something away from them, they cannot get it back from it. How feeble are both the seeker and the sought! They do not measure Allah with His true measure. Allah is Strong, Almighty."*
>
> (22: 73-74)

This challenge from Allah to all creation has been an enduring and continuing one over fourteen centuries and will continue until the end of the world without any human being being able to meet it and create even a single fly, that insignificant creature which Allah Almighty has used in His challenge to mankind. This challenge is is not confined to any specific time, people, group, or race. Allah Almighty called upon the scholars and scientists of the entire world to accept the challenge and assist one another and support one another in creating a single living cell. But even now, although they can achieve many things in every field of science, they have not been able to meet that challenge.

The challenge remains

Thus there is a challenge which has stood since the Revelation of the Noble Qur'an which no one has been able to meet because it comes from Allah Almighty. The more time passes, Allah brings greater challenges to mankind because over time, faith weakens, people's attachment to science increases, and their self-delusion by their intellects increases. Allah Almighty makes clear to us the fruits of their science in relation to Divine Power.

Some may wonder whether the Qur'an will become weak at the end of time as faith has become weak. The answer is no. Faith will grow weaker but the Qur'an's power will remain. We see even now that although people's faith has diminished the Qur'an has retained its power. There are people who are engaged in publishing elegant copies of the Qur'an adorned with gold ink, and everyone is eager to possess one or more copies of the Qur'an in his house, in his car, or in his work-place. It may well be that if you investigate, you will find that many of them have not read it even once in their entire life. There are even non-Muslims involved in publishing sumptuous editions of the Qur'an. There are people who can write the entire Qur'an on a single page. Qur'ans are published in Japan, Italy and Germany.

All that is happening now so that Allah Almighty has subjugated non-Muslims to publishing the Qur'an in a form which befits the majesty of its words. It is amazing to see non-Muslims in the service of the publication of the Qur'an while those who believe in the Qur'an are not working to publish it! The position of the Qur'an will be strengthened because it is protected by Allah Almighty. It is faith that is weakening as time passes. One might suppose that the opposite would be the case and that the perceptions of man and his learning some of the secrets and laws of existence which Allah has disclosed to him would impel him to greater awareness of his Lord. This brings us to some more words of the Almighty:

> *"The likeness of the life of this world is that of water which We send down from the sky, which then mingles with the plants of the earth to provide food for both people and animals. Then when the earth is at its loveliest and takes on its fairest guise and its people think they have it under their control, Our command comes upon it by night or day and We reduce it to dried-out stubble, as though it had not been flourishing just the day before. Thus do We make Our Signs plain for people who reflect."* (10:24)

In this noble *ayat* Allah Almighty presents us with a simile for the life of this world from its beginning to its end. Allah Almighty compares the life of this world to the water which falls from heaven. Without it there would be no life on the earth. If the rain were withheld then all on the earth would die – humans, plants and animals – and the earth would become a bare desert, a dead place. The means of life, then, all come from heaven. Water descends, pure and purifying, and mixes with the earth; it gives people what they eat and what their flocks eat. It gives them food and water and what they need to preserve their lives. Then people begin to adorn the earth, and all that is on the earth is an adornment for it. As Allah Almighty says:

> *"We made everything on the earth adornment for it so that We might test them to see whose actions are the best."* (18:7)

We must turn to the text of the noble *ayat*. Why did Allah Almighty not say, "An adornment for you"? Because no one can own all that is on the earth. It remains on the earth until Allah inherits the earth and those on it. Thus people's ownership is only metaphorical: they are merely caretakers of what they pretend to own. For instance, I may say that I own this building but in fact after I depart from this world it will be transferred from hand to hand to many other people. Each of them claims to be its owner but then he leaves it and goes and yet another "owner" comes.

So all the adornment on the earth and its orchards and gardens and the buildings which people have been skilful in building in a beautiful and attractive fashion – all this is an adornment which is enjoyable so that no one can prevent people looking at it. The truth is that we do adorn the earth and the adornment of the earth increases whenever man advances in science and discovers new means to utilise the earth's resources. This will happen for generation after generation until Allah inherits the earth and those on it.

To summarise, we may say that there is no "how" with Allah Almighty. When He says, "Be!" the thing is. But as science advances, people think that they control the earth and its contents and they can do what they want with it. Then the command of Allah will come to destroy all of this and the Reality will appear to every human being. It will not appear like the invisible things in which we are asked to believe but as witnessed facts when the end of the world comes.

Chapter Six
We Recognise the Truth

Because Allah has disclosed to man a few of the secrets of existence, man's overweening arrogance and self-delusion have made him imagine that he has the power to make life proceed in accordance with his wishes and his management. He deviates far from the Path of Allah and makes his own laws. This is utter ignorance and delusion without any foundation whatsoever. Now we hear cries of ignorance asserting that the Age of Faith has ended and the Age of Science has begun.

Man has been able to fill the earth with things which previous ages did not know about, and every day he is given new knowledge which adds to human comforts and amenities; but man fails to ascribe any of the basic essentials and necessities of life to their true Source.

We must understand well that the human being is not solid and deeply-rooted in existence. He is a transient visitor who comes and lives for a limited period of time and then his life ends. A human lifetime bears no relation to the life-span of this world: the life-span of this world is hundreds of thousands or millions of years. This should not distract us from the important fact that what matters us is our own period of life on this earth, which is most unlikely to exceed a hundred years.

The stability of the universe gives us an illusory feeling in two ways. Firstly it makes us feel that this existence has no end. Whatever people say about the end of the universe, you will find that everyone who lives in it believes that it will be millions of years before existence comes to a end. Secondly we have the illusion that the things which serve us in existence give to us of their own accord. This is an illusion, since in reality they give to us only by the power and permission of Allah Almighty. Everything in this universe is continually subject to the Power of its Creator. Nothing happens in the universe created by Allah which is outside of what Allah wills to happen. Man can only adorn the earth through the powers which Allah has lodged in it. All that is on the earth is its adornment as Allah Almighty says:

> *"We made everything on the earth adornment for it so that We might test them to see whose actions are the best. We will certainly make everything on it a barren wasteland."* (18:7-8)

So all that is on the earth and that you see is the adornment of the earth itself, and you can enjoy the adornment of the earth as long as you are on it. When your life ends your enjoyment of the adornment will end. You will leave, but the earth will remain with its adornment. One day the command of Allah will come and this world will end. The universe and all the adornment on the earth will become rubble and everything will end.

When Allah Almighty finds that man has deluded himself and abandoned His Path, despite the Signs He has given him which confirm that the only Creator is Allah, then the life of this world has failed to teach the lesson it was appointed to teach. In that case it only remains for Allah Almighty to acquaint man with the reality he has failed to grasp. It is as if He were telling him, "Your self has deluded you and you have put yourself far from the Path, believing that you live by virtue of your own efforts. So I will now acquaint you with the truth." Here we must point out the meaning of the noble *ayat* quoted above:

> *"Its people think they have it under their control."*
> (10:24)

They do not really have it under control – it is just opinion and supposition and is not the truth. They do not control it, but merely imagine they do: it is self-delusion. Then Allah Almighty will come and change what appeared immutable in this world by the application of His power, which has no limits or restrictions.

The End of the World as depicted by the Noble Qur'an

Allah informs us about some of the Signs which will succeed one another and pave the way for the end of the world. He says in *Surat at-Takwir*:

> *"When the sun is compacted in blackness, when the stars fall in rapid succession, when the mountains are set into motion, when the camels in foal are neglected, when the wild beasts are all herded together, when the oceans surge into each other, when the souls are arranged into classes, when the baby girl buried alive is asked for what crime she was killed, when the Pages are opened up, when the Heaven is peeled away, when the Fire is set ablaze, when the Garden is brought up close: then will each soul know what it has done."* (81:1-14)

When will these phenomena take place? They will occur when Allah Almighty reveals to the earth and to all existence that the time has come for it to end. Then it will only be only moments before all existence is destroyed and comes to an end. The Almighty also says:

> *"When the earth is convulsed with its quaking, and the earth disgorges its charges, and man asks, 'What is wrong with it?', on that Day it will impart all its news because your Lord has inspired it. That Day people will emerge segregated to see the results of their actions. Whoever does an atom's weight of good will see it, and whoever does an atom's weight of evil will see it."* (99:1-8)

Revelation or inspiration (*wahy*) is the conveying of information by a concealed means from a source to the person to whom it is given. No one understands it but the Revealer and the one to whom it is revealed. Allah Almighty reveals whatever He wishes to whomever He wishes. Inspiration is not confined to the Messengers but it embraces many creatures. Allah Almighty revealed to His Messengers, but He also revealed to Musa's mother, as we read in the words of the Qur'an:

> *"We revealed to Musa's mother, 'Suckle him and then when you fear for him cast him into the sea.'"* (28:7)

He inspired the bees, as He says:

> *"Your Lord inspired the bees: 'Build dwellings in the mountains and the trees, and also in the structures which men erect.'"* (16:68)

Allah also inspired the Disciples of 'Isa ibn Maryam, peace be upon him. In the words of the Almighty:

> *"When I inspired the Disciples to believe in Me and in My Messenger."* (5:111)

Inspiration can also come from others than Allah, as Allah Almighty says:

> *"The shaytans inspire their friends to dispute with you."*
> (6:121)

But the Revelation of Divine Law from Allah Almighty comes only to the Messengers He has chosen to receive it.

When the end of the world comes, Allah Almighty will inspire something in the earth. Some people think that the earth is inanimate and insensate. How can Allah inspire anything in it? The fact is that the Almighty Creator has given all of His creatures a language which they speak but which we do not necessarily understand. The Creator understands it and the creature itself understands it. We find in the Qur'an that Allah Almighty says:

> *"There is nothing which does not glorify His praise, but you do not understand their glorifying."* (17:44)

This means that everything in existence celebrates the praise of Allah and worships Him; but because of our limited knowledge we do not hear nor understand this glorification. The Almighty says:

> *"We subjected the mountains to Da'ud, glorifying, and the birds as well."* (21:79)

Beware of assuming that the creatures which you see around you are inferior to you in perception or consciousness. These creatures may have more knowledge than you. The ant understood that when the armies of Sulayman passed, they would trample on their colony. That is why it shouted out a warning to the rest of the ants that they should enter their houses to flee from the troops and to save themselves from being trampled. Read what Allah Almighty says:

> *"Then, when they reached the Valley of the Ants, an ant said, 'O ants! Enter your dwellings so that Sulayman and his troops do not crush you unwittingly.'"*(27:18)

How did this ant know that it was Sulayman and his armies who were passing overhead? From where did he learn that? How he did he know that when Sulayman and his armies passed they would trample on the valley of the ants? How did this ant understand that if the ants entered their dwellings they would be safe from being crushed? The ant must have had knowledge or understanding which made it aware of all of this. We do not know all this but we belittle the ant because of its small size and the ease with which it can be eliminated.

Read what the hoopoe said to Sulayman, peace be upon him, as the Noble Qur'an reports:

> *"However, it was not long delayed and then it said, 'I have comprehended something you have not and bring you from Sheba an accurate report. I found a woman ruling over them who has been given everything. She possesses a mighty throne. I found both her and her people prostrating to the sun instead of Allah. Shaytan has made their actions appear good to them and debarred them from the Way so they are not guided and do not prostrate to Allah, Who brings out what is hidden in the heavens and the earth, and knows what you conceal and what you divulge. Allah — there is no god but Him — the Lord of the Mighty Throne.'"* (27:22-26)

How did the hoopoe comprehend what Sulayman did not comprehend, in spite of the fact that this noble Prophet had been given a kingdom which had not been given to any other human being? Who told the hoopoe that that land was Sheba, that the ruler of the land was a woman, and that she was a queen and had a mighty throne? Who told it that she and her people were worshipping the sun rather than Allah, that this is disbelief, that Shaytan was the one who had made their actions appear good to them and had debarred them from the Way, and that that was the reason why they were not guided? Who informed the hoopoe that worship should be directed to Allah alone, that Allah owns the kingdom of the heavens and the earth, and all that this noble *ayat* reports it as saying? How did the hoopoe understand that, when we say that it has no intelligence?

These and other things which are reported in the Noble Qur'an affirm that there is knowledge which the creatures of Allah have but which mankind does not know; and that they can discriminate and understand. Allah Almighty has given them what enables them to perform their task in existence. As that applies to animals, birds and insects, the earth and heavens also hear and speak. Read the words of the Almighty:

> *"Then He turned to heaven when it was smoke and said to it and to the earth, 'Come willingly or unwillingly.' They both said, 'We come willingly.'"* (41:11)

Allah Almighty spoke to the heavens and the earth, and the heavens and earth replied after hearing the words of Allah Almighty. The Almighty says about this:

> *"When the sky bursts open, hearkening to its Lord as it is bound to do. When the earth is flattened out and disgorges what is inside it and empties out, hearkening to its Lord as it is bound to do."* (84:1-5)

The meaning of the word of the Almighty "hearkening" is hearing with the ear. Where are we in respect of this ultimate knowledge of the universe? Yet when Allah Almighty has disclosed to us just a very few of the laws of existence, we appropriate them to ourselves and suppose that existence is subject to us by our will. We think that we can do whatever we want with it, and that we can command existence and it will obey us. When we reflect on this noble *ayat*, however, we find that there is an ultimate knowledge in existence which is veiled from us – and that what we know is actually very little indeed.

When man worships his own intellect

When man disbelieves in his Lord and worships his intellect and believes that he controls existence, the command of Allah Almighty will come and destroy every familiar thing in existence. Man's feeling of power over the earth will be shown to be a complete delusion and all that is familiar will come to an end. The sun will rise from the west; it will then be obliterated

71

and its light go out. The familiar constellations of stars will disappear and the stars will collide together and fall. The same will be true of the mountains on the earth, which will be scattered from their locations. Allah Almighty says on this subject:

"They will ask you about the mountains. Say: 'My Lord will scatter them as dust.'" (20:105)

The mountains' mass will evaporate and they will be like carded wool. The full picture of what will occur at the end of the world is that the familiar world we know will disappear. That with which you are familiar serves you, but it does so only serves you because Allah has subjected it to you. Allah will end its subjugation and it will no longer be at your service.

The earth which used to give you crops and fruits which you eat will not give you anything. The mountains, which are the pegs of the earth to preserve its stability and ensure people's nourishment, will be scattered. The sun, too, which gives warmth and light and permits life in existence, will no longer undertake its task; its task will have ended. The adornment of the earth that you had thought you had achieved and would last forever will depart and be removed from you. All of this will end. This world of means will vanish and come to an end. Even your own control over yourself will vanish and come to an end.

Your feet will no longer be subject to you for you to walk onn them wherever you wish. They will obey their Creator Who put them at your disposal and made them obey your will. Your hands, which you used will no longer be under your control and will no longer be prepared to obey your instructions. Indeed, all the parts of the body which Allah Almighty subjected to your will will no longer be subject to you. You will go wherever Allah wills, even to Hell. Your tongue will only speak when Allah wishes. Your eyes will only see when Allah wishes them to see and without any command on your part. That is why there are those who will be blind when gathered on the Day of Rising, even though they could see in this world. It is

72

only Allah Almighty Who gives eyes the power to see in this world and it is He Who will strip them of that power in the Next World. People thought that they were living by their own power, walking by their own power and talking by their own power. But Allah Almighty, Who gave them that power, can and will remove it from them. The same applies to everything around us. All that you are familiar with in this world will change.

All this applies to those who are alive at the end of the world. But what about those in the grave? Will those who are in their graves when the world ends experience the same kind of change? The answer is yes, because it marks the beginning of a new stage for all. Their bodies will be returned to them and their spirits will return to their bodies. They will emerge from the ground and the life of the Interspace which they experienced throughout their period in the grave will depart from them. Allah Almighty indicates to us that our stay in the grave is not forever but for a determined period after which man will emerge from it. The Almighty says:

*"Fierce competition for this world has distracted you until you **visit** the graves."* (102:1-2)

Note that the Almighty said "visit". He did not say, "Be forever" or "remain". The meaning of "visit", as we know, is to go to a friend or relative for a period of time. You remain with him for however long it may be, and then leave. If you take up residence with him you are no longer a visitor. Whether your visit is long or short, it will end. If this term is applied to the dead it shows that those who inhabit the graves, from Adam until the end of the world, are only "visitors" to their graves. They will spend some time in them and then leave them.

Will those who have died since the time of Adam remember the time they remain in their graves? The answer is no, because when Allah asks people after they leave their graves how long they have been there they will think that they have been there for very little time.

> "On the Day the Last Hour comes the evildoers will swear they have not even tarried for an hour. That is the extent to which they are deceived. Those who have been given knowledge and belief will say, 'You tarried in accordance with Allah's Decree until the Day of Rising. And this is the Day of Rising but you did not know.'" (30:55-56)

So in the life of the Interspace man does not feel time. Time is the measure of events, and there are no events there – and so there is no sense of time. All those who have died are waiting in a Book which my Lord does not lose or forget. Allah Almighty has counted them and numbered them exactly. None of them will be left behind on the Day when people stand before the Lord of the Worlds.

How will people's bodies be restored?

Some people may ask how people's bodies will be restored as they were. How is it possible for individuals to be restored as they were after their bodies have rotted away? Allah Almighty replies to them:

> "As We originated the first creation so We shall regenerate it." (21:104)

This is something easy for Allah Almighty because it is He Who brought things into existence from non-existence and created them without any prior model. He brought them into existence in the life of this world when they did not exist at all, and so it is still easier for Him to restore them in the Next World, since that is bringing back into existence something which has already existed. We use "easier" metaphorically for the sake of the human mind because there is no question of ease or difficulty for Allah Almighty. Rather everything is simple and there is nothing of which He is incapable, in either the heavens or the earth.

Each human body is distinct from all others, which is why the cells of a human body recognise one another by an individual code or language which Allah Almighty teaches it. So when a human being, for instance, sustains a major injury, the rest of the cells of the body reproduce and multiply until it is mended and is restored to the same shape as it had before. But if you bring the limb of one body and attempt to transplant it into another body, you will find that it rejects it and does not accept it. How can the body distinguish between what is part of it and what is from a different body, when all bodies are very similar? Each body must have an individual code which distinguishes it from all other bodies and is never duplicated. So when we want to transplant limbs successfully, the recipient of a transplant must take drugs and medicine which prevent or reduce the efficacy of this code so that it does not reject this alien element which is transferred from another body.

Similarly, everybody has a distinctive individual smell which we ourselves cannot distinguish, but some animals – dogs, for instance – can. That is why when a dog smells a handkerchief or a personal item, it can pick out the owner from hundreds of individuals. There are in fact dozens of distinguishing factors which enables you to identify one individual among hundreds of individuals.

When Allah Almighty gives us this knowledge as a mercy to our intellects, it enables us to understand that when the spirits return to the bodies, the bodies which they had lived in will be restored in such a manner that each is distinct from all other bodies which have existed from the time of Adam to the end of the world.

Man and the elements of the earth

It is true that all of us are created from the elements of the earth. Each of us, however, has a distinct form which differs from all other forms; so the proportion of the elements in the body is not the same even if the elements are the same. All of us contain the sixteen elements which exist in the earth, but the proportion varies in each and every one. To make that easier to grasp, we can take the colours of paint as an example. There are countless different hues of a single colour. If we take white, for instance, and put one or two drops of yellow in it, it becomes a different colour. When we add any quantity, we change the colour. When we take red and add one or two drops to the mixture, it is different. When we put seven or eight drops, it is different again. The regulation of colours is a very fine and precise operation because every addition of any colour results in a new colour.

Man was created from the elements of the earth, which, as I said, number sixteen basic elements. An increase of even an atom of these elements gives a different human being, and a decrease gives a different human being. By the power of Allah Almighty, the permutations yield an infinite number of possibilities.

Thus we see that a fundamental change occurs to man at the end of the world, but there is one thing in which we will nearly all share: the swooning which will affect every living creature except those whom Allah wishes. Allah Almighty says:

> *"The Trumpet will be blown and all in the heavens and all in the earth will lose consciousness, except those Allah wills."*
> (39:68)

When the world comes to an end and man's science, which he supposed would give him control over the earth, ends, people will know the reality and recognise that their knowledge was a very superficial knowledge. This is in accordance with the words of Allah Almighty:

"No indeed, if you only knew with the Knowledge of Certainty, you will certainly see the Blazing Fire! Then you will certainly see it with the Eye of Certainty." (102:5-7)

At that point people will recognise true knowledge. After this knowledge which Allah Almighty gives us – the "Knowledge of Certainty" in the life of this world – it will become "the Eye of Certainty." There are the Knowledge of Certainty, the Eye of Certainty, and the Truth of Certainty. What is the difference between them? We say that the knowledge which we take from Allah Almighty is the Knowledge of Certainty because it issues from Allah Almighty. The believer is certain that it will actually occur and it is as if he sees it directly in front of him. Allah Almighty says:

"They know an outward aspect of the life of this world but are heedless of the Next World." (30:7)

So it appears that the knowledge which we receive from Allah Almighty is the Knowledge of Certainty, and that then later when we see the Unseen after the spirit leaves the body, whether it is in the interspatial life or on the Day of Rising, our direct visual experience of it is the Eye of Certainty, meaning that we see it directly in front of us with our own eyes. After the Reckoning, vision then becomes the Truth of Certainty, because for those who enter the Fire and are in it it is the Truth of Certainty that they experience and feel it; and it will be the Truth of Certainty for those who enter the Garden, because they experience its bliss after they have seen it.

That is how when the world comes to an end, every falsification in man's knowledge will end and man will see before him everything in its reality, without falsehood and in complete certainty. He will see the angels, he will see the shaytans, he will see the Garden and he will see the Fire. He will recognise the Immensity of his Creator – Majestic and Exalted is He! He will know with absolute certainty that there is no power and no strength in this existence except through Allah – glory be to Him and exalted is He!

This world will end with its suns, moons and stars. A new earth will be illuminated by the Light of its Almighty Lord. Then the Book will be set in place and the Balance will be set up, and every soul will be repaid in full for what it did after the termination of the world of means. We will then be in the presence of Allah, the Causer of all causes.

These are some of my reflections about the end of the world. I ask Allah to give us success and guide us to the Straight Path.

DAR AL TAQWA LTD

Publishers
Booksellers
Distributors
Printers & Stationers

BOOKS PUBLISHED BY DAR AL TAQWA LTD.

TITLE		NO.PAGES	PRICE
1. THE MIRACLES OF THE QURAN By Sheikh M. Al-Sharawi ISBN 1 870582 01 2	HBK PBK	276 276	£12.95 £6.50
2. THE SIGNS BEFORE THE DAY OF JUDEGEMENT By Ibn Kathi ISBN 1 870582 03 9	PBK	96	£3.95
3. THE JINN IN THE QURAN AND THE SUNNA By Mustafa Ashour ISBN 1 870582 02 0	PBK	66	£3.95
4. THE ISRAA AND MIRAJ THE PROPHET'S NIGHT JOURNEY AND ASCENT INTO HEAVEN By Abdul Hajjaj ISBN 1 870582 06 3	PBK	56	£3.95
5. THE SOUL'S JOURNEY AFTER DEATH By Layla Mabrouk ISBN 1 870582 05 5	PBK	40	£2.95
6. YASIN AND AL-RAHMAN TRANSLATED + TRANSLITERATED ISBN 1 870582 00 5	PBK	44	£1.50
7. PART THIRTY OF THE HOLY QURAN ARABIC, TRANSLATED AND TRANSLITERATED ISBN 1 870582 00 5	PBK	102	£1.95
8. JEWELS OF GUIDANCE By Hamza M. Salih Ajjaj ISBN 1 870582 00 4	PBK	88	£3.95
9. THE WORLD OF THE ANGELS By Sheikh Abdul Hamid Kishk ISBN 1 870582 00 6	PBK	96	£3.95
10. FATE AND PREDESTINATION By Sheikh M. Al-Sharawi ISBN 1 870582 07 1	PBK	80	£3.95
11. DIALOGUE WITH AN ATHEIST By Mustafa Mahmoud ISBN 1 870582 09 8 (Published May 1994)	PBK	180	£5.50

7A Melcombe Street, Baker Street, London NW1 6AE
Telephone: 020 7935 6385 / 6690 Facsimile: 020 7224 3894
www.daraltaqwa.com

DAR AL TAQWA LTD

**Publishers
Booksellers
Distributors
Printers & Stationers**

TITLE		NO.PAGES	PRICE
12. THE INTERPRETATION OF DREAMS By Ibn Sirin ISBN 1 870582 08 X (Published May 1994)	PBK	160	£5.95
13. HOW ALLAH PROVIDES By Sheikh M. Al-Sharawi ISBN 1 870582 10 1 (Published June 1994)	PBK	96	£3.95
14. MAGIC AND ENVY By Sheikh M. Al-Sharawi ISBN 1 870582 11 X (Published July 1994)	PBK	78	£3.95
15. GOOD AND EVIL By Sheikh M. Al-Sharawi ISBN 1 870582 25 X (Published August 1994)	PBK	74	£3.95
16. THE LAWS OF MARRIAGE IN ISLAM By Sheikh M. Rif'at Uthman ISBN 1 870582 30 6 (Published March 1995)	PBK	104	£4.95
17. THE ISLAMIC WILL By Hajj Abdal Haqq + Aisha Bewley Ahmad Thomson ISBN 1 870582 35 7 (Published April 1995)	PBK	68	£5.95
18. DEALING WITH LUST AND GREED **ACCORDING TO ISLAM** By Sheikh 'Abdul al-Hamid Kishk ISBN 1 870582 40 3 (Published June 1995)	PBK	145	£5.95
19. TEACH YOUR CHILDREN TO LOVE **OF THE PROPHET** By Dr. Muhammad Abdu Yamani ISBN 1 870582 45 4 (Published June 1995)	PBK	76	£3.95
20. THE WATER OF ZAM ZAM By Muhammed Abd al Aziz Ahmad Majdi as-Sayyid Ibrahim ISBN 1 870582 55 1 (Published March 1996)	PBK	53	£3.95

**7A Melcombe Street, Baker Street, London NW1 6AE
Telephone: 020 7935 6385 / 6690 Facsimile: 020 7224 3894
www.daraltaqwa.com**

DAR AL TAQWA LTD

Publishers
Booksellers
Distributors
Printers & Stationers

TITLE		NO.PAGES	PRICE
21. PORTRAIT OF HUMAN PERFECTION By Shaykh Ahmad Muhammad Al-Hawfi ISBN 1 870582 50 0 (Published March 1996)	PBK	128	£5.95
22. YAJUJ AND MAJUJ Muhyi-d-din Abd Al-Hamid ISBN 1 870582 60 8 (Published Novermber 1996)	PBK	41	£3.95
23. MUHAMMED (SAW) Dr. Mustafa Mahmoud ISBN 1 870582 70 5 (Published March 1997)	PBK	68	£3.95
24. AL MAHDI AND THE END OF TIME Muhammed ibn Izzat Muhammed Arif ISBN 1 870582 75 6 (Published May 1999)	PBK	74	£3.95
25. THE DAY OF RISING Laila Mabrouk ISBN 1 870582 85 3 (Published September 1997)	PBK	183	£5.95
26. DUNYA THE BELIEVERS PRISON, THE UNBELIVERS PARADISE Muhammad Abd Ar Rahman Iwad ISBN 1 870582 802 (Published October 1997)	PBK	160	£5.95
27. CIRCUMCISION IN ISLAM Abu Bakr Abdu'r Razzaq ISBN 1 870582 95 0 (Published August 1998)	PBK	120	£5.95
28. JOURNEY THROUGH THE QURAN THE CONTENT & CONTEXT OF THE SURAS Muhammad al-Ghazzali ISBN 1 870582 90 X (Published August 1998)	HBK	580	£25.00
29. PART 29TH OF THE QURAN ARABIC, TRANSLATED & TRANSLITERATED ISBN 1 870582 11 X (Published October 1998)	PBK	128	£2.95

7A Melcombe Street, Baker Street, London NW1 6AE
Telephone: 020 7935 6385 / 6690 Facsimile: 020 7224 3894
www.daraltaqwa.com

DAR AL TAQWA LTD

Publishers
Booksellers
Distributors
Printers & Stationers

TITLE		NO.PAGES	PRICE
30. PART 28TH OF THE QURAN ARABIC, TRANSLATED & TRANSLITERATED ISBN 1 870582 16 0 (Published October 1998)	PBK	96	£2.96
31. DIVINE EXISTENCE VERSUS DOUBT Shaykh Muhammad M.\al-Sha'rawi ISBN 1 87 0582 26 8 (Published February 1999)	PBK	64	£3.95
32. THE HEART & THE TONGUE THEIR SICKNESSES AND CURES Sheikh Yassin Roushdy ISBN 1 870582 21 7 (Published February 1999)	PBK	48	£3.95
33. ALLAH THE DIVINE NATURE Yassin Roushdy ISBN 1 870582 31 4 (Published February 1999)	PBK	120	£5.95

7A Melcombe Street, Baker Street, London NW1 6AE
Telephone: 020 7935 6385 / 6690 Facsimile: 020 7224 3894
www.daraltaqwa.com